Self-Discipline

Everyday Habits

and Exercises

to Build Self-Discipline

and Achieve Your Goals

By Martin Meadows

Download another Book for Free

I want to thank you for buying my book and offer you another book (just as long and valuable as this book), *Grit: How to Keep Going When You Want to Give Up*, completely free.

Visit the link below to receive it:

http://www.profoundselfimprovement.com/dailyselfdiscipline

In *Grit*, I'll share with you exactly how to stick to your goals according to peak performers and science.

In addition to getting *Grit*, you'll also have an opportunity to get my new books for free, enter giveaways, and receive other valuable emails from me.

Again, here's the link to sign up:

http://www.profoundselfimprovement.com/dailyselfdiscipline

Table of Contents

Download another Book for Free......................... 2

Table of Contents 3

Prologue 6

Chapter 1: Fundamental Keys
of Self-Discipline 9

    Commitment's Best Frenemy: Adversity...... 13

    Exercise: Boost Your Motivation
    with This Simple Trick.................................. 14

    How to Build an Unwavering Belief
    in Success... 16

    FUNDAMENTAL KEYS OF SELF-
    DISCIPLINE: QUICK RECAP 19

Chapter 2: Physical Excellence Leads
to Mastery in Life... 21

    Habit: Follow a Workout Plan Religiously ... 24

    How to Never Quit Your Fitness Program.... 29

    Side Mission: Win Against Yourself 36

    Habit: Maintain a Healthy Diet 38

    How to Stick to Your Diet Despite
    Uncontrollable Cravings 41

    Side Mission: Try Intermittent Fasting 52

Habit: Wake Up Early (or Go to Sleep at Regular Hours) 55

PHYSICAL EXCELLENCE LEADS TO MASTERY IN LIFE: QUICK RECAP 59

Chapter 3: Discomfort Builds Character 63

Exercise: Get Comfortable with Cold Temperatures 66

Exercise: Do Without Something You "Need" 68

Exercise: Rejection Therapy 71

Exercise: Failure Therapy 72

Habit: Do the Most Difficult Things with No Hesitation... 74

Exercise: Learn Something Difficult............. 76

DISCOMFORT BUILDS CHARACTER: QUICK RECAP 94

Chapter 4: Live with Intent 97

Habit: Sharpening Your Awareness with Quiet Repose 98

Exercise: Embracing the Tunnel Vision...... 107

Exercise: Talk with Your Future Self 110

Exercise: Build Your Compass 112

LIVE WITH INTENT: QUICK RECAP 114

Chapter 5: Burnout and Discouragement

– It's Not All About Self-Discipline 117

   Stretch Yourself, but Don't
   Break Yourself 119

   Positive Mindset Is Essential for Mental
   Toughness (and Vice Versa) 122

   How Focusing on Negativity Can Ruin Your
   Self-Discipline... 126

   What to Do When You're Stuck in a Funk or
   Suffer from Negative Self-Talk 128

   BURNOUT AND DISCOURAGEMENT
   – IT'S NOT ALL ABOUT
   SELF-DISCIPLINE: QUICK RECAP 133

Epilogue 136

Download another Book for Free..................... 139

Could You Help?... 140

About Martin Meadows 141

Prologue

I haven't always been a disciplined person. In the past I couldn't follow even the simplest routines. I had an unhealthy diet, exercised little (and hence, was overweight), and didn't have the discipline to commit to the process of changing myself.

Today, I follow a strict routine. I have a morning routine, go to the gym three times a week and regularly practice several other sports including tennis, cycling, and swimming. I maintain a healthy diet and constantly work on new, challenging goals to become a better person.

It took me years before I finally understood what discipline is and how to apply it in my situation. Now I'd like to share what I've learned with you.

In my first book about self-discipline, *How to Build Self-Discipline: Resist Temptations and Reach Your Long-Term Goals*, I approached the subject of building self-discipline from the perspective of developing impulse self-control.

In this book you will learn the ins and outs of building long-term, daily self-discipline rather than just situational willpower. While *How to Build Self-Discipline* was more focused on techniques to deal with specific problems, *Daily Self-Discipline* is about turning yourself into a person who becomes more self-disciplined with each day – and can successfully use this skill for personal growth.

In addition to discussing tips to help you grow self-discipline, we'll also discuss various ways to become a mentally stronger person. If you find it difficult to keep pushing in spite of obstacles, or if you feel you lack willpower to continue when motivation runs out and discomfort kicks in, *Daily Self-Discipline* is for you.

As in all my books, I spend little time discussing theory, instead sharing with you practical exercises you can implement in your life. Consider this book a menu out of which you can pick various techniques to see which one tastes best for you (and produces the best results).

Each chapter is summed up with a quick recap to help you better remember what you've just read, so you can have a quick refresher whenever you go back to each section.

To avoid repeating disclaimers throughout the book – please exercise caution whenever following any of my tips – particularly the ones related to your health.

I'm not a doctor, nor a psychologist, nor a priest, nor anyone with formal credentials to tell you what you should do with your life. I'm not qualified to make any decisions for you or give you any health recommendations – particularly if you suffer from chronic conditions such as diabetes, hypertension, or mental illness of any kind (including mild depression).

Chapter 1: Fundamental Keys of Self-Discipline

Would you like to succeed when dieting instead of being yet another person who has failed?

Would you like to become a successful businessman instead of a wannabe entrepreneur?

Would you like to become a world-class performer instead of a mediocre jack-of-all trades?

It all starts with committing yourself to the process and having an unwavering belief your plan is going to work out.

Dieting is a perfect example of how powerful commitment is.

In a paper written by Rena R. Wing and Suzanne Phelan[i], the authors point out that despite "a general perception that almost no one succeeds in long-term maintenance of weight loss, research has shown that ≈20% of overweight individuals are successful at long-term weight loss when defined as losing at least

10% of initial body weight and maintaining the loss for at least 1 year."

They also cite the example of the members of the National Weight Control Registry who have lost an average of 73 pounds (33 kg) and maintained the loss for more than 5 years.

Their secret? Commitment.

These individuals reported engaging in high levels of physical activity (on average at least one hour a day), eating a low-calorie diet, monitoring their weight, and maintaining a consistent eating pattern across weekdays and weekends. There was nothing magical about their diets.

As the authors of the paper emphasize, after these individuals have successfully maintained their weight loss for 2–5 years, the chance of longer-term success is greatly increased.

What happens in those two to five years that makes the success more likely? It's the moment when you develop long-term self-discipline, which is the result of following your plan day in, day out.

When I was 21, I was over 30 pounds overweight. When I finally realized I couldn't go on like that, I picked a diet that made sense to me (it was a slow-carb diet by Tim Ferriss[ii]) and stuck to it for several months. It was the first time I tried losing weight.

I learned the guidelines and followed them to a T – including the mandatory cheat day at the end of every week (and mind you, I took it seriously; you wouldn't believe the amount of food I inhaled each cheat day and still lost weight every single week).

Unlike the majority of first-time dieters, I was successful right away. I didn't have to try ten different diets. I achieved my goal in about three months. I never went back to my old physique again. Just like the subjects of the study, maintaining healthy weight became easy once I changed my habits and stuck to them.

Why didn't I need to try dozens of diets before finally losing weight?

Because I understood that it didn't matter which diet you follow (as long as it's not a ridiculous single-food diet), but whether you stick to it and believe in its effectiveness.

From the weight loss point of view, the key is not the diet. The key is your ability to adhere to a specific diet and follow it until you achieve your intended outcome. I was also lucky to blindly believe my diet would work. I wasn't tempted to try any other diet. My certainty ensured I didn't have to jump from one diet to another to achieve my goal.

A crucial thing to underscore here is the belief that my diet would work. Would I have the discipline and determination to keep going if I wasn't sure about the end goal? I doubt it. When you combine belief with commitment, you get the perfect mixture.

This approach to dieting can be applied in every other area of life by understanding it's not what you do, but whether you do it consistently and with an unwavering belief until you reach your objective.

I applied the same approach to self-confidence, learning languages, sports, saving money, writing, and business. The most important principle –

commitment – became a crucial source of my self-discipline and my special sauce for achievement.

However, commitment isn't always easy. In fact, more often than not we have to face doubt and obstacles more than a few times before we reach our goals. And that's why we need to learn how to deal with another "A" – adversity.

Commitment's Best Frenemy: Adversity

You don't need self-discipline when things go smoothly. After all, what can tempt you to give up if you're winning?

Few people give up dieting on the first day or stop their workout schedules in the middle of the first workout.

It's only when things get more difficult, when you no longer have the initial motivation, that you lose discipline and determination. People who are capable of dealing with adversity are better prepared to win against their weak side and keep going despite the temptation to give up.

And how do you become better at handling adversity? You introduce it in your life and befriend it. When you become more comfortable with unfavorable circumstances, you'll be able to handle them better.

The purpose of this book is to share with you habits and exercises to build your mental toughness, and consequently the ability to flourish even when faced with adversity.

Your self-discipline will grow as a result of putting yourself in unfavorable situations and going past them. You'll also become more determined and motivated, because pushing through obstacles and reaching goals despite them will teach you the mindset of a winner.

Exercise: Boost Your Motivation with This Simple Trick

There's an old adage originating in the writings of 11th century Persian Sufi poets. They tell the story of a powerful king who asks wise men to create a ring that will lift his spirits when he's sad. The sages hand him a ring with the words "This too will pass" etched on it[iii].

Abraham Lincoln incorporated the story in his address before the Wisconsin State Agricultural Society in Milwaukee on September 30, 1859:

"It is said an Eastern monarch once charged his wise men to invent him a sentence, to be ever in view, and which should be true and appropriate in all times and situations. They presented him the words: "And this, too, shall pass away." How much it expresses! How chastening in the hour of pride! How consoling in the depths of affliction![iv]"

Each time you feel discouraged when trying any of the exercises or habits described in this book, use this simple trick to realign your perspective.

Whether you're facing adversity because you've put yourself against it voluntarily (by, say, forcing yourself to wake up at six in the morning) or due to unforeseeable circumstances, reminding yourself that everything eventually passes is a powerful trick to aid you in enduring the discomfort.

I use this trick regularly to keep myself centered – no matter what happens, I remind myself it's temporary and the tide always eventually changes. It sounds simplistic, but it works – just try it.

How to Build an Unwavering Belief in Success

While you can never attain 100% certainty that you'll achieve your goals (doubt is always there, even if never voiced), you can take some steps to become more confident in yourself and get more disciplined, too.

The trick is to watch what others have done to accomplish the same goal and imitate them. By following a proven plan, you'll get rid of a lot of uncertainty coming from following a rarely traveled path.

If there are hundreds or thousands of people who have followed a specific plan and achieved success, there's nothing standing in your way of achieving it.

If your goal is to lose weight, follow a diet with lots of genuine before/after photos and stories.

If you want to build a business, learn from experienced entrepreneurs who have helped hundreds of other new businessmen.

If you want to acquire a certain difficult skill, learn it from someone who has a lot of experience teaching it (and ideally, a lot of experience with learning in general so she can better relate to your situation).

The knowledge that you're learning from someone who has achieved the same goal will reduce your self-doubt – after all, you'll be traveling a proven path, and not just wandering like a child lost in the woods.

When you combine this belief with commitment and proper mindset ("this too shall pass"), you'll have the basic tools to start building an iron-like resolve to keep going no matter the circumstances.

All ideas shared in this book will help you in the long term. The goal is to boost your baseline self-discipline, and not just give you a momentary feeling of self-control because you overcame one little temptation.

With these fundamental keys in mind, let's move on to more specific exercises and habits you can introduce in your life to develop your own discipline.

Please keep in mind the objective of these exercises is self-discovery – helping you find out what works for you in terms of building self-discipline and what doesn't.

FUNDAMENTAL KEYS OF SELF-DISCIPLINE: QUICK RECAP

1. The fundamental keys of self-discipline are commitment (adhering to a specific plan until you achieve your goal) and belief that your long-term plan is going to work out.

2. You don't need self-discipline when things go smoothly. It's only when plans go south you get tempted to give up. Consequently, you need to train yourself to handle adversity. The best way to become more capable of dealing with unfavorable circumstances is to purposefully put yourself in them – which is what this book is all about.

3. Whenever you feel that adversity is too much to handle, remind yourself that "this too shall pass." Every challenge in life is a temporary thing. You can handle more than you believe if you remind yourself that things will soon get better.

4. You need an unwavering belief in your plan to make commitment easier. Ideally, follow proven advice coming from a credible person with lots of real-world experience. For instance, when losing

weight, pick a diet that has made thousands of people slim. In the case of building a business, follow an outline provided by a successful entrepreneur, ideally in the industry you'd like to follow. When learning a new skill, follow the action plan laid out by an experienced teacher.

Chapter 2: Physical Excellence Leads to Mastery in Life

Few people are better examples of self-discipline and commitment than professional athletes.

What an average person sees when she looks at an elite performer – say, a world-class tennis player – is that his abilities seem natural, easy. She concludes, "He was born with it. It was given to him."

And she couldn't be farther from the truth.

What she sees is an event – the act of winning. What she doesn't see is thousands of hours of practice. His sore body, countless hours of drills, lost matches, and everything else that has made him the tennis player he is today.

He had never been born with his abilities, and neither is anyone else. It's the result of a long process taking years or decades, not mere days or weeks.

A part of his achievement might have something to do with his innate talent – physical strengths like great hand-eye coordination. However, if it wasn't for the daily self-discipline to bring out those strengths, he would never have become a world-class tennis player.

Working on your physique to increase your speed, strength, or flexibility is a perfect introduction to the world of building self-discipline. You won't achieve any of these goals without dedication, long-term planning, and determination.

According to research conducted for Centers for Disease Control and Prevention, 34.9% of US adults are obese[v]. In other words, it's safe to say a large part of the Western world has never had much experience with sports for long enough to develop strong habits of self-discipline and persistence. If they had, they probably wouldn't be obese, because developing these traits generates permanent lifestyle changes that aren't obesity-friendly.

Charles Duhigg, author of *The Power of Habit*[vi], calls regular physical activity a keystone habit – capable of introducing several more positive habits as side effects of the first change. A study by Steven N.

Blair, David R. Jacobs Jr. and Kenneth E. Powell shows[vii] that regular physical activity may lead to reduced overeating, smoking, alcohol consumption, and risk taking. By adding physical activity to your daily routine, you can develop these positive side habits almost automatically.

For this reason, physical excellence is an essential part of building a disciplined life. And no, I'm not talking about becoming a world-class athlete or a perfectly sculpted human being. Constantly working on your health and fitness – to your capabilities and genetics, not comparing yourself to others – is what builds a great deal of discipline in life.

You can't build a strong body in a few months, which makes it a perfect activity to add as one of your daily self-discipline building habits. When you adhere to a specific routine for months or years on end and you start seeing the results, you can't help but learn to respect the process. It's when you switch from the event-oriented to the process-oriented life when the magic happens.

As MJ DeMarco, bestselling author of *The Millionaire Fastlane: Crack the Code to Wealth and Live Rich for a Lifetime*[viii], writes in his book, "Success demands your focused exercise into the journey and the tools of that journey (process) as opposed to the destination (event)."

Habit: Follow a Workout Plan Religiously

Gym attendance (or any other kind of fitness activity done on a regular basis) is a useful indicator of how disciplined you are.

A meta-analysis conducted by Ryan Rhodes at the University of Victoria in British Columbia and Gert-Jan de Bruijn at the University of Amsterdam[ix] shows that among the people making fitness-related New Year's resolutions, 46% of them quit by June.

Gym Membership Statistics by International Health, Racquet & Sportsclub Association[x] show even worse numbers – 67% of people with gym memberships never use them. The gyms actually make more money on people who don't use them than the ones who do.

Let's guess how disciplined these people are…

There are two pieces of the puzzle at play to achieve an ideal physique. The first one is physical activity. The second one – arguably more important – is maintaining the proper diet.

Both regular physical activity and a healthy diet require a dose of daily discipline. When you follow these two habits daily, you'll build a powerful source of discipline you'll be able to use to achieve other goals in your life.

Let's start with physical activity. Since this is not a fitness book, I won't give you an exact plan to follow. Just like there's no perfect plan when dieting, there's also no perfect plan for exercise.

The only requirement is to introduce some kind of a tracking system in your weekly schedule and stick to it. For instance, you'll exercise on average an hour a day, and do it no matter what. Neither weather, laziness, nor your friends coming over for a weekend will deter you from exercising.

I'm partial to weightlifting and other anaerobic types of exercise that can build muscle and help you achieve a stronger, good-looking physique (and that applies to both men and women – dear ladies, don't be afraid you'll get bulky).

Anaerobic exercise is characterized by short duration (up to 2 minutes[xi]), high intensity activities that lead to increased strength, speed, power, and muscle mass.

Good choices here include:

- weightlifting – as already mentioned, it's probably the best choice for most people due to its ability to develop your entire body in perfect harmony (contrary to a popular image, proper weightlifting isn't about building huge biceps, but about building a strong body with healthy proportions)

- sprinting –particularly hill sprints, which are safer for joints, more effective for fat loss, and much more demanding than regular sprints on flat terrain[xii].

- swimming – when done in short, high-intensity bursts of activity instead of an hour-long marathon.

- yoga – can be a healthy way to build a well-rounded lean body for both genders. Maintaining uncomfortable poses is, in itself, a great discipline-building exercise.

- calisthenics (body weight exercises) – can be a perfect replacement for weightlifting if you constantly progress to more difficult exercises.

All of these sports support building a balanced, muscular, and healthy body. Getting these results is crucial in developing your discipline. Progress and reward will fuel your efforts to keep going despite setbacks, though ideally, most of your motivation should come from within – regardless of the results.

In addition to anaerobic activity, it's good to introduce some variety to your workouts and perform some aerobic activities as well.

I do them mostly not for the health benefits (which are still obviously important), but for the enjoyment and the stress-reducing effect they provide (just note it takes at least 10 weeks of regular exercise to experience significant changes to your stress levels[xiii]).

It's all connected with discipline as well – a relaxed individual has a much easier time resisting temptations and sticking to his plan than an overstressed person.

Here are a few ideas for aerobic exercises which are a lot of fun and provide incredible health benefits:

- cycling – long rides can be demanding not only physically, but also mentally, which makes it a perfect sport for building self-discipline.

- walking or jogging – simple, easy, cheap, and runner's high[xiv] feels good.

- tennis – arguably one of the most difficult sports requiring a lot of self-discipline to master even the basics.

- inline skating – a fun exercise that almost doesn't feel like exercise.

- swimming – when not done in short bursts of high-intensity activity. One of the best types of activities for obese individuals (swimming is lighter on your joints than, say, jogging).

- martial arts – a huge aspect of martial arts is the mental development, which makes it a perfect holistic exercise.

How to Never Quit Your Fitness Program

The five most common reasons why people quit their fitness programs (and subsequently lose self-discipline) are:

1. The wrong kind of motivation

There are two kinds of motivation: internal and external.

Denis Coon, best-selling author in the field of psychology defines internal motivation (also known as intrinsic motivation) as something that occurs "when we act without any obvious external rewards. We simply enjoy an activity or see it as an opportunity to explore, learn, and actualize our potentials"[xv].

External motivation, also known as extrinsic motivation, is defined by sports psychologists Peter Terry and Costas Karageorghis as motivation that can come "from the outside, such as the motivation to win medals, receive financial rewards, and attract attention from the media. This is known as external, or extrinsic, motivation because it involves participation in sport for some kind of reward that is external to the process of participation"[xvi].

The type of motivation you need to stick to your fitness program and build your self-discipline is intrinsic motivation. Just like you shouldn't build your self-discipline solely because you want to impress somebody, you shouldn't go to the gym only because you think someone will praise you or admire you for it.

If you work out primarily because you expect a certain reward and draw little to no personal enjoyment or fulfillment by doing it, reconsider your motivation.

You build your self-discipline when you keep doing something simply because it helps you realize your full potential and not because it will make you look good in the eyes of other people or provide you with rewards.

If you can't seem to find intrinsic motivation, try a different, more enjoyable sport that will encourage you to explore, learn, or actualize your potential. If you hate it, you won't do it in the long term, anyway. Speaking of which, the second reason is…

2. Lack of enjoyment

Having a lot of discipline is great, but it doesn't mean you have to always choose things you don't like (don't confuse it with doing things that are uncomfortable for the purpose of growth).

In 1997, researchers at the University of Rochester and the University of Southern Utah conducted a study on intrinsic motivation and exercise adherence[xvii]. One group of participants participated in Tae Kwon Do classes while the other group attended aerobics classes.

The first group had better adherence than the second one because they focused on enjoyment, competence, and social interaction. In other words, they chose participating in a type of fitness class they enjoyed and not a class that was focused specifically on helping them achieve their fitness goals.

Both choices could have been equally uncomfortable for them (if they weren't used to regular physical exercise), but it was Tae Kwon Do that they enjoyed more – and that's the same approach you should follow whenever making changes that are uncomfortable in themselves (like exercising more or changing your diet).

If you don't enjoy your fitness plan, change it. Try to pick at least one of each type of exercise – anaerobic and aerobic. If you go to the gym, nobody says you have to use this or that machine – there are various ways of achieving the same goals (although a simple approach with free weights is usually the most optimal[xviii]).

If I recommend aerobic exercises, it doesn't mean you have to go to a class at your local gym. In fact, I'm against it because I can't imagine a more boring way to exercise than spending an hour in a room doing jumping jacks and other nightmarish exercises I remember from my PE classes.

Have fun when moving. Play tennis with a friend. Jog with your dog. Go on a bike ride and explore your surroundings. Have a kayaking trip with a group of friends. The less it feels like exercise, the easier it will be to make it a permanent part of your life.

3. Lack of support

It's great to have enough self-discipline to achieve your goals without the help of others. However, it doesn't mean it's the best way of doing things. In fact, support from other people can often make or break your resolutions.

A study conducted by Brandon C. Irwin at the Michigan State University and his colleagues shows that exercising with a partner improves performance on aerobic exercises[xix]. A different study conducted by the same researchers suggests that working out with a slightly better partner makes individuals more persistent[xx].

It's due to the Kohler's effect[xxi], a phenomenon wherein a person works harder as a member of a group than when working alone. If you can work harder and develop better discipline when working with a group, why not benefit from it and get support?

4. Wrong expectations

Regular physical activity improves your self-discipline by teaching you two things: how to adhere to a specific plan and how to be patient when waiting for the results. If you start your workout plan with the wrong expectations, though, it's likely you'll quit before you improve your mental toughness.

Due to the phenomenon of the false hope syndrome (making frequent attempts at self-change while holding unrealistic expectations about the likely speed, amount, ease, and consequences)[xxii], you're likely to set unrealistic goals and expect things that can't happen in a specified time frame. To avoid discouragement, research what kind of results you can expect realistically and set them as your goals. When building self-discipline, small wins are more important than aiming for the stars and not even landing on the Moon.

5. A lack of time

A lack of time is usually the least legitimate reason to quit a fitness program because it masks a different kind of a problem. If you can't find time to take care of your body, then the problem isn't your lack of time, but your lack of priorities. Few people would disagree that health is the most important thing in life, yet the lives of many people don't reflect it.

In this case, you need discipline to identify your values, and most importantly, design your life in such a way that it will reflect them. If health is one of your primary values in life (and it should be, because everything else matters little if you don't feel well), sacrifice one of your lesser values (say, climbing the corporate ladder) for it.

To give you an example from my life, I have several rules regarding the types of businesses I can run. For instance, I purposefully avoid hiring full-time employees because the benefits of increased earnings potential can't outweigh the health-affecting drawbacks (adding a lot of stress to my life).

I could probably make more money acting against my rules (after all, most entrepreneurs agree you can achieve much more if you have a team of full-time employees), but my health is more important to me than material wealth, so I'm fine with this tradeoff.

What kind of tradeoffs do you have in your life, and do they reflect your own values?

Do you value family and health over your career, yet spend 60 hours a week working with no real plan to reduce your workload? Perhaps it's time to figure out how to change the work-family time ratio.

If you avoid these five most common reasons, you'll have a much easier time sticking to your workout routine, and consequently, building lasting self-discipline. Don't forget, though, that all of these problems are there to help you become tougher – it's your job to figure them out, not use them as excuses why you should give up.

Side Mission: Win Against Yourself

You build willpower primarily when you don't feel like doing something but do it anyway. In the case of working out, it means going to the gym and lifting weights (or doing your sprinting/swimming high-intensity routine) despite a lack of energy or motivation.

Each day I feel tired, weak, and generally not ready for a workout, I remind myself it's the most important workout day for me. That's when my discipline is truly tested and when it strengthens – if I win against my weaknesses.

If you can perform a workout despite a light cold (if your symptoms are mostly "in your head" exercise is fine[xxiii]), hangover, general bad day, or any other weak excuse, you're already ahead of the pack. These small wins build up and strengthen your resolve like a muscle. If you can do it consistently for years, you probably have enough discipline to achieve anything you want in life.

Now, don't misunderstand and act in spite of your body (I'll talk more about it in a later chapter). If you've been experiencing negative symptoms for days, don't be stupid. Stop working out, figure out what's wrong (not enough rest, too much stress, a lingering illness, etc.), and return when you're ready.

To avoid burnout, take a weeklong break every 3 months or so. A Japanese study on training and detraining led by Riki Ogasawara has shown that even three weeks off isn't enough to compromise the progress at the gym[xxiv].

In the study, one group of participants was forced to take three weeks off while the other group kept their regular 3x per week training schedule. At the beginning of week nine, the first group resumed their training schedule.

When scientists measured results after 15 weeks, the progress was equal for both groups. In other words, strategic breaks won't affect your results negatively and can provide a welcome period of rest providing both psychological and physical benefits.

As an additional benefit, a break (and subsequent return to your regular regimen) will test your self-discipline. For people with weak resolve, it's more difficult to get back to the gym after a break, so it's a good way to see how strong your fitness habits are.

If you feel restless during your week off and look forward to going back to the gym, it's safe to say you have developed a strong discipline of working out regularly.

Habit: Maintain a Healthy Diet

In today's world, few things in life are more difficult for most people than maintaining healthy weight. There are temptations everywhere – billboards advertising cheap fast food, your favorite snacks discounted at the store, friends asking you out to grab a bite in a burger joint, or simply a pizza a phone call away, delivered in 30 minutes or less.

Fortunately, obesity is not something people are born with. Except for a few legitimate medical conditions (and it doesn't apply to over 99% of people, so you probably can't use it as an excuse), the only reason why people are obese is their lack of self-discipline.

Controlling your weight is not optional – it's mandatory if you want to become a self-disciplined person. At the risk of sounding politically incorrect, you're unlikely to achieve success in other areas of your life if you can't deal with excess pounds.

As life coach Peter Sage puts it in his video "3 Things All Successful People Do"[xxv], "if you don't make time for health, you'll have to make time for illness." How self-disciplined and successful can you be when your body refuses to serve you? And note it's not an "if," it's a "when" if you don't care about your health.

And these are not the words coming from a person who has been slim his entire life. I, too, was overweight and take full responsibility for who I used to be. I had the wrong beliefs about nutrition and the wrong personal values – putting enjoyment from eating over my health. Moreover, it was my conscious decision not to educate myself how to change it.

Now, that doesn't mean I'm a proponent of following a radical diet consisting of bland foods. You can enjoy your meals and still be a healthy, vibrant human being.

Which diet should you follow for best results? There's no right answer.

Dr. David Katz at Yale University's Prevention Research Center and his Yale colleague Stephanie Meller compared various popular diets such as a low carb diet, low fat diet, low glycemic diet, Mediterranean diet, mixed/balanced (DASH) diet, Paleolithic diet, vegan diet, and elements of other diets[xxvi].

Surprisingly (or not, depending on how you look at it), they found no winner. Every diet was associated with health promotion and disease prevention as long as it was "of minimally processed foods close to nature, predominantly plants."

If you focus mostly on unprocessed foods and stick to them, your body will change. And when these new habits become a way of living for you (not a diet, but a lifestyle), you'll notice changes in other aspects of your life, too.

You'll get more energy – which you'll want to use to spend more time doing something active which positively affects your wellbeing. You'll have more mental clarity, which will help you learn new things and grow as a person. Plus, you'll develop a better work ethic, which will help you stick to your new resolutions and achieve your objectives more easily.

How to Stick to Your Diet Despite Uncontrollable Cravings

The biggest challenge with changing your eating habits is shifting from your old, unhealthy ways to the new, more beneficial ones.

There's no denying most people just can't deal with the overpowering feeling of hunger (even if it's only been a few hours since their last meal) or the feeling of longing to eat an unhealthy meal.

While eliminating entire groups of foods permanently from your life is not an optimal approach (after all, eating is a large part of pleasure in life and you shouldn't deprive yourself of it by never eating anything less than 100% healthy), it's necessary to learn how to deal with food cravings so you can develop more control over your body.

A person who can say no to a powerful craving is the person who will be more likely to say no when feeling tempted to give up or choose laziness over working on her goals.

I give more detailed tips on how to deal with cravings in my book, *How to Build Self-Discipline: Resist Temptations and Reach Your Long-Term Goals*. Meanwhile, here are three quick tips that will help you deal with cravings better:

1. Distract yourself

In the famous Stanford experiment on delayed gratification, children were offered a choice between a small immediate reward (a marshmallow, a cookie, or a pretzel) or two small rewards 15 minutes later[xxvii]. During the waiting period, the tester left the room, leaving children with the alluring reward tempting them at their fingertips. Some kids gave up and ate the reward right away; others waited and received two rewards.

The subsequent follow-up studies have shown that the children who were able to resist the temptation were found to be more successful in life (as measured by SAT scores, incidence of behavioral problems, and BMI)[xxviii].

How did the kids deal with the temptation, especially when taking into account the general lack of self-discipline among children when compared to adults? They distracted themselves.

As the leading researcher Walter Mischel observed, some would "cover their eyes with their hands or turn around so that they can't see the tray, others start kicking the desk, or tug on their pigtails, or stroke the marshmallow as if it were a tiny stuffed animal."

While it doesn't really sound like a great strategy to stroke the chocolate bar or kick your desk each time you're tempted to cave in, the general idea behind it – self-distraction – is.

Removing temptations from sight is the simplest and most effective strategy. If you don't have any forbidden foods at home, it will be easier to resist the temptation to cheat.

There's a difference if there's a chocolate bar on your shelf vs in a store 15 minutes away. The same applies to any other temptation-generating elements of the environment such as TV (ads), driving nearby to your favorite fast food restaurants, etc.

Waiting on the temptation for fifteen minutes is usually enough to greatly diminish the craving. If it's still there, keep distracting yourself (instead of trying *not* to think about the temptation, try to focus on something else entirely) until it passes.

It's useful to develop a default habit to do in place of eating unhealthy foods. For instance, each time you feel the temptation to drive to the nearby pizza joint, grab your shoes and racket and head out to the local tennis court. Soon, the less-than-helpful part of your brain will forget about the temptation and focus on the other activity.

As the hot-cold empathy gap says[xxix], we generally find it difficult to understand how it feels to be in an opposite state. If we're satiated, it's difficult to understand how hunger can take over our control. If we're angry or sad, it's difficult to understand how it feels to be happy. If we aren't sexually aroused, we fail to predict the kind of risky sexual decisions we can take while being in the "hot" state[xxx].

In the case of craving for unhealthy food (say, mac and cheese), it's difficult to imagine that eating it will *not* be delicious. It's only when you give in that you can experience the emotion you would have never expected during your "hot" state (then you find it hard to believe you couldn't have resisted the temptation given how unsatisfactory the experience turns out to be).

Then there are also other negative effects of giving in to a craving like how upsetting a certain food can be for your stomach or how quickly the taste can go from incredible to horrible. It's difficult to think of these consequences when you're in the "hot" state, so it's important to be realistic about the craving by pondering all of the potential outcomes.

Instead of (yet again) being puzzled as to why you imagined your forbidden food as so great (and finding out it's not really that incredible, and you only get guilt as a reward), think about it prior to making the wrong decision. Logic doesn't always work to avoid these wrong decisions (after all, it's an emotional craving), but it can help.

2. Don't make it too difficult

It's useful to be a self-disciplined person, but it doesn't mean you should make everything as difficult as possible just so you can improve your willpower. The easier dieting is, the less likely you'll be to cave in to a temptation and give up.

In my case, having a designated cheat day every week let me know I only had to postpone my cravings for a few days. I wasn't required to give up my favorite unhealthy foods forever – it was just for a few days. With time, I stopped craving these foods so much, so in the end, taking the easy way out (cheating each week) was better than making things too challenging (not allowing myself any cheating).

Science also agrees cheat meals are valuable. Overeating (while on a low-calorie diet) helps increase the levels of leptin production by nearly 30% for up to 24 hours[xxxi]. This post-cheating increase in leptin, which regulates body weight, boosts metabolism and may also lead to improved motivation[xxxii].

Unfortunately, only high-protein, high-carb, and low-fat cheat days affect the levels of leptin[xxxiii]. In other words, if your sole purpose of cheating is to boost your leptin levels, you have to say no to pizza, ice cream, chocolate, and other fatty foods. Doesn't sound like a happy cheat day, does it?

However, it doesn't mean you have to strictly control your cheat days. There are both physiological and psychological effects of cheating. Even if you can't obtain the maximum physiological benefits because you choose not to have a low-fat day, you can still enjoy the psychological ones.

Giving yourself a scheduled break will save you guilt. Instead of entering the vicious post-guilt cycle ("I already screwed up, it doesn't make sense to get back on track") – which will surely happen, because few people can adhere to a strict diet with 100% accuracy – incorporate cheating into your diet.

It's about long-term commitment, not depriving yourself of everything and hoping you'll fight off every single temptation. As long as you maintain healthy eating habits 80-90% of the time, you'll be fine. Both your health and self-discipline will improve the longer you stick to a healthy diet – even with occasional returns to less healthy foods.

3. Change your cravings

People succumb to cravings not only because they miss eating pizza, hot dogs, ice cream, or french fries. They also cave in because they never develop permanent alternatives to them.

Unless you develop an enjoyable alternative to the unhealthy foods you love, you'll always miss them so much that resisting cravings will be very difficult. Can you guess how easy it is to maintain a diet that lets you eat all that you want? The key is to find healthy alternatives that give you what you want (that normally comes from unhealthy foods).

And let's be honest here – you can't replace the perfect, sweet taste of chocolate melting on your tongue with a stalk of bland broccoli. However, you can probably do it (to some extent – enough to not miss chocolate every single day) with:

- all kinds of berries (strawberries, raspberries, blueberries – is there anyone who doesn't love them?),

- dark chocolate (it's much healthier, and due to its deep taste – we're talking about 70% cacao content here – you need much less to satisfy your sweet tooth),

- smoothies (just don't go overboard with it – that's a lot of fructose),

- high-quality honey (there's a world of difference between cheap store honey and homemade organic varieties – experiment with various flavors)

- carob (while not entirely something you can eat on a daily basis as a healthy alternative, it's better than regular chocolate)

Some types of unhealthy foods can be made healthier by using healthier ingredients. For instance, pizza can be made whole-wheat with homemade tomato sauce and a high-quality cheese. You can eat natural frozen yogurt and mix in some berries instead of eating store-bought ice cream. You can make homemade french fries instead of buying oil-coated frozen ones.

Spices and herbs also have a lot to do with taste. Many vegetables rarely taste good alone. However, if you add the right spice or herb to them, they get much tastier – oftentimes so tasty, you develop a craving for these foods. To give you a few examples, here are spices and/or herbs that dramatically change the taste of certain healthy foods:

1. Eggs: chives, salt, and/or black pepper. Scrambled eggs alone can be a bit bland. Adding any of these makes the taste much better.

2. Zucchini: cayenne pepper, basil, cumin, garlic powder, oregano, or thyme. A lot of herbs and spices go well with zucchini. Few people enjoy this vegetable alone, but adding just a pinch or two of any of these flavor-intensifiers can make a world of difference – especially if you grill it.

3. Brown rice: turmeric, cumin, or soy sauce. Most people used to eating white rice are not as happy with the taste of brown rice. Try combining it with turmeric or cumin, or add soy sauce. You can also check Asian spice mixes for rice.

4. Vegetable soups: salt, black pepper, allspice, bay leaf, and/or garden lovage. Also, add a lot of onions to improve the flavor. Simple, everyday vegetable soups are perfect for anyone who doesn't like cooking every single day. You can make a big pot of soup on Monday and eat it until Thursday.

With the right mix of spices, you can certainly develop a craving for soup (like I have).

5. Potatoes: salt, rosemary, paprika, oregano, basil, cayenne pepper, dill, and/or parsley. Potatoes, when eaten in moderation and not in the form of french fries, aren't as unhealthy as people believe. The key is to avoid frying them, instead opting for healthier methods, ideally by steaming. Once you come up with your perfect mix of herbs and spices, steamed potatoes might become more appealing than oil-coated french fries.

Experimentation can go a long way to avoid, or at least greatly reduce, cravings for certain foods. Once you develop permanent alternatives you find as tasty (or tastier) than what you have craved, maintaining your healthy eating habits will get easier. It will also be a great lesson in creative self-discipline – going around a temptation or eliminating it altogether rather than caving in.

Side Mission: Try Intermittent Fasting

Intermittent fasting (IF) is a pattern of eating in which you periodically fast for a specified number of hours. Most people follow a basic form of intermittent fasting every day. Unless you wake up at night and eat, each day you fast for at least 8 hours. That's why the first meal during the day is called a "breakfast."

Proponents of intermittent fasting suggest fasting for longer – usually at least 16 hours a day. Other approaches include alternate day fasting (eating what you want one day, and not eating anything the next day), 24-hour fasts (say, you stop eating at 6 PM and resume eating at 6 PM the next day), and 40-hour fasts (by skipping an entire day of eating).

I've already talked about IF in a few of my previous books (most notably, *How to Relax*), so I won't repeat myself here to address the most common questions and doubts[xxxiv]. The only disclaimer I have to leave here is that intermittent fasting is not for everyone. If you suffer from any health conditions, speak with your doctor first.

Having said that, most healthy people should have no problems skipping an entire day of eating, or just a meal or two. It's a beneficial thing for your health and your self-discipline.

Hunger is an interesting feeling to handle. If you're used to eating every three or four hours, you'll feel hungry every three or four hours. It doesn't matter whether you've eaten enough calories for the day or not – your body's signals follow your habits.

And here's when willpower comes into play. At first, it's uncomfortable to feel hunger and not give in. You'll be tempted to grab something to eat, but instead you'll let this feeling pass and continue your fast.

The goal is to teach yourself how to stay disciplined despite an uncomfortable feeling. Just like having a regular workout routine is uncomfortable at first and you feel tempted to get instant gratification (spend your day in front of the TV instead of going to the gym), so will fasting test your willpower.

It takes a certain kind of discipline and toughness to go without food for longer periods of time, but with enough experience, hunger becomes a non-issue (or at least, less powerful than it used to be).

Try fasting once or twice and see how it makes you feel. Perhaps you can make it a part of your daily or weekly routine to change your relationship with food and learn how to control your urges better.

If you love eating, but can still go without food for 40 hours, few things will pose a challenge to your willpower.

Habit: Wake Up Early (or Go to Sleep at Regular Hours)

If you wake up and go to sleep every single day at about the same time and feel well-rested, you can probably skip this part. If you feel your sleep schedule requires some work, working on this aspect of your life will improve your health as well as help you build more self-discipline.

There's an important caveat regarding waking up early. While it's generally perceived that waking up early is a virtue, a habit everyone who wants to become successful should develop, science doesn't necessarily agree.

In fact, a German study on chronotypes shows that the brains of early risers are different than the brains of night owls[xxxv]. In other words, waking up early isn't always optimal for you if you're predisposed to staying up late.

However, don't use that as an excuse for waking up late if you don't feel well following your normal sleep schedule. For a long time, I used to go to bed at 3 or 4 in the morning and wake up at 2 PM. I could have argued I was a night owl, but I never felt particularly well-rested. When I went from one extreme to another – waking up at 6 AM – I learned that early rising was a more optimal choice for both my energy and general productivity.

There are two general approaches to waking up early. If your goal is to wake up at 6 AM, you can either set your alarm for 6 AM right away and take it from there or wake up a minute or two earlier each day until, usually after at least a few weeks, you reach your goal.

I prefer the cold turkey approach. It's a difficult test for your self-discipline, but produces results more quickly. Even if you slip up a few times, you can change your internal clock in a matter of a week or two instead of several weeks.

Few things test your self-discipline more than the alarm clock forcing you to leave your comfortable, warm bed and start a new day – especially if you're starting it with something you don't particularly enjoy. That's why waking up early is a perfect exercise to build mental toughness and learn how to overcome your weaknesses.

If waking up early is a particularly difficult goal for you – as it was, and sometimes still is for me – consider increasing the stakes.

It can be something as simple as scheduling something for the morning that you absolutely can't miss (so it will provide motivation to avoid hitting the snooze button) or as deliberate as placing a bet with your friend (if you don't wake up at 6 AM, you'll pay him $20 or whatever is painful enough to you that it will motivate you to get up).

For instance, I have foreign language lessons in the morning. Even if I don't feel like waking up early (as it sometimes happens), my body will wake me up right before the lesson.

It takes a lot of willpower to unlearn the habit of staying up late and hitting the snooze button several times before getting up. Once you permanently change your sleep schedule and start regularly waking up early, you'll experience a powerful shift in self-discipline. You'll develop your own tools to stick to your resolutions even when you're still half-asleep and susceptible to choosing the easy way out.

If you're not an early riser, you can introduce a habit of going to sleep and waking up at regular hours (but please test your hypothesis and spend at least a month following an early morning routine). It also requires daily self-discipline, helps you better structure your day, and optimizes your body (it gets confused if you wake up and go to sleep at random hours).

PHYSICAL EXCELLENCE LEADS TO MASTERY IN LIFE: QUICK RECAP

1. Regular physical activity is a keystone habit, which means it positively affects other areas of your life, helping you make several beneficial changes by only introducing one.

2. Becoming a fit and healthy person is one of the best things you can do to build your self-discipline. It requires patience and dedication to the process, which are the two things you need to develop in order to enjoy higher levels of willpower.

3. Exercises can be either anaerobic (high-intensity, short duration) or aerobic (lower intensity, longer duration). For optimal results, choose at least one anaerobic and one aerobic type of activity.

4. To overcome the five most common reasons why people quit their fitness programs, develop intrinsic motivation (coming from within you, not the rewards you expect), find exercises you enjoy (because building self-discipline isn't about making your life permanently miserable), consider working out with a partner (because accountability helps stay

on track), have the right expectations, and make your routine reflect your personal values (so you make time for exercise).

5. Whenever you don't feel like working out, remind yourself that it's a test of your self-discipline. If you resist the temptation to get lazy, you'll get rewarded with a fulfilling (though possibly more demanding than usual) training that will develop your toughness.

6. If you don't make time for health, you'll have to make time for illness. Getting rid of excess weight is not optional – it's mandatory if you want to become self-disciplined and grow in other areas of your life.

7. If you're struggling with cravings, learn how to shift your focus from the temptation to something else. Don't keep any forbidden foods at home. Whenever you have a craving, give yourself something else to do for fifteen minutes as it will probably reduce in intensity if you only wait. Come up with healthy habits that will replace your usual routines whenever you feel a craving (e.g. going on a walk instead of driving to the nearest pizza joint). Be

realistic about the potential negative consequences of giving in to a craving – when you eat a certain unhealthy food, it won't feel as good as you think it will when you crave it.

8. Don't be afraid to schedule cheat days or cheat meals so you have something to look forward to. It will only make dieting easier, and still help you achieve your goals. Always think about the long term perspective – if you can't imagine sustaining your current eating habits for the rest of your life, you're probably too restrictive.

9. You won't deal with cravings if you don't develop permanent, healthy, and enjoyable alternatives to the foods you crave. Don't rely on your self-discipline only – get creative and find ways to satisfy your cravings without actually succumbing to them.

10. Intermittent fasting is a good way to test your ability to choose postponed gratification over instant rewards. Skip eating from time to time to reconnect with the uncomfortable feeling of hunger.

11. Making a change to wake up early is one of the most difficult tests for your self-discipline because we're usually the most susceptible to giving in to temptations in the morning when we're still groggy and half-asleep. Test different waking hours to see how they affect your mood (and also to see whether you can overcome your weaknesses).

Chapter 3: Discomfort Builds Character

It was a partly sunny summer day. I went with my friend to a nearby lake to kayak. The surface was still and the sun shone on us. We rented kayaks and went on our merry way.

Thirty minutes later, blue skies turned into a dark, menacing dome of clouds. Wind rocked our kayaks. Paddling got more and more difficult as waves formed on the surface of the lake. And then the heavy rain came, soaking us within minutes.

With blisters on our fingers, we fought our way back. The waves crashed against my kayak and continuously turned it into the wrong direction. My shoulders and hips were tense and exhausted within a few minutes of rapid paddling.

And yet, despite what seemed like a nightmarish turn of events, I felt exhilarated. Like a madman, I laughed and grunted to the rhythm of the wild paddling. Even when the waves rocked the kayak so much I was afraid I would go into the water, I still enjoyed the experience. Even a fresh, pink, burning blister on my thumb didn't ruin my mood.

Fifteen minutes later, the skies cleared up and the sun shone on us again. We paddled back to the shore, smiling and laughing at the wild experience despite our sore bodies.

It hasn't always been like that for me. I learned how to feel confident despite discomfort and draw pleasure out of it thanks to conscious practice. When I mastered how to appreciate the challenges for what they were – great adventures and opportunities to grow – my life got easier. Indeed, life's easier when you live it the hard way.

How comfortable do you feel with discomfort? Have you ever experienced an uncomfortable situation and laughed in spite of it? Do you seek inconvenience or stay as far away from it as possible?

Discomfort is a part of human nature. For thousands of years, humans lived in dire circumstances, fighting for survival every single day.

It's not in spite of the obstacles, but thanks to them that we thrive today.

If nature hadn't tested us, we wouldn't have developed ways to protect ourselves against it. Despite modern conveniences, life today is still similar to what it used to be. Any bad things we experience in our daily lives make us stronger and more prepared to deal with similar problems in the future.

If you didn't scrape your knees as a kid and get yourself a few bruises, how capable of dealing with pain would you be today?

Seneca, Epictetus, and Marcus Aurelius, three famous proponents of Stoicism all proposed imposing mild self-discomfort to prepare oneself for possible adversity and to develop more appreciation of the things one takes for granted.

Professor William B. Irvine writes in his book, *A Guide to the Good Life: The Ancient Art of Stoic Joy*[xxxvi] that "pursuing pleasure, Seneca warns, is like pursuing a wild beast: On being captured, it can turn on us and tear us to pieces. Or, changing the metaphor a bit, he tells us that intense pleasures, when captured by us, become our captors, meaning that the more pleasures a man captures, 'the more masters will he have to serve.'"

If you purposefully refuse to serve some of your "masters," you'll grow more capable of dealing with adversity. Nobody lacks mental toughness when the circumstances are perfect. Your self-discipline is only tested during times of adversity. If you make it a regular habit to put yourself in tricky situations, you'll be better prepared to deal with them when they happen without your voluntary involvement.

Exercise: Get Comfortable with Cold Temperatures

Exposing yourself to cold temperatures is one of the simplest ways to learn how to handle discomfort. The simplest, most insightful exercise is taking a 5-minute cold shower. And no, don't just count 5 minutes in your head – set a stopwatch and don't leave the shower until 5 minutes pass. Don't cheat – turn the knob all the way to cold.

The period of two months I spent taking two ice-cold 5-minute showers a day was one of the most helpful things I did to increase my mental toughness.

The first time I took a cold shower, my entire body was numb. I struggled not to jump out of the shower after the first hit of water. Several showers later I become more attuned to the feelings of discomfort, discovering that the first two minutes were the most difficult. After two minutes passed, suddenly things became much easier and I knew I could stand the cold without that much difficulty.

I then applied the same learnings in other aspects of my life, reminding myself that the first steps usually test your self-discipline the most. If you can handle them, you can handle much more than you think.

That's the kind of a lesson the exercises in these books are for. You can only learn them on your own. When you discover exactly when and how you're tempted to give in and what helps you handle discomfort, you'll become more capable of dealing with postponed gratification.

I won't say you should take cold showers every day. Two months after I started taking cold showers, I went back to regular hot showers. I learned my lessons. It makes little sense to make yourself miserable on a daily basis to feel you're tough.

Another exercise to test your mental toughness is to go out underdressed for the weather. Obviously, you shouldn't do it when you're sick or when you're going to explore the wild outdoors. However, going for a walk once or twice without a jacket, with only a thin sweater on, can be a valuable experience for building mental toughness. Just be reasonable about it – we're talking about slight discomfort here, not putting yourself in a situation where you can get frostbite or hypothermia.

Exercise: Do Without Something You "Need"

There are certain things and habits you need in your everyday life to feel comfortable. It can be carrying your smartphone everywhere you go, checking your email ten times a day, drinking coffee first thing in the morning or sleeping in your warm, comfortable bed.

As an example, instead of sleeping in my own bed I chose to sleep on the balcony of my apartment a few times. It's a simple, easy thing most people (with balconies and backyards, at least) can do to experience brief discomfort and stop taking their comfortable bed for granted.

What if you're addicted to your smartphone and absolutely can't leave it at home for the fear of not replying soon enough to a message from your friend? You guessed it – leave it at home for a few hours and observe how you feel without it. Stay with your anxiety and go past it – nothing bad will happen, and you'll only get tougher by getting rid of one of your "necessities" for a while.

Below are a few more examples of doing without something you "need."

1. Walk to work instead of driving. In many cities it's not practical to do, but that's precisely why it's a great self-discipline building exercise.

2. Go camping, ideally away from any facilities so you're forced to wash or do other hygiene-related activities without modern conveniences.

3. Do a 24-hour email fast. During these 24 hours, don't check your email at all. Don't do it if you're waiting for an important message or can't afford it because your job requires it – that's not the point of this exercise. You can try it when you're on vacation, but still check your email out of habit.

4. Replace your evenings in front of the TV with educational reading (non-fiction books about skills and goals you'd like to achieve.)

5. Live like a miser for a week or two. Avoid every single unnecessary expense. Don't buy new food – eat leftovers, canned food, and all of the bland foods you rarely eat that just sit there in your fridge or pantry. Don't buy any new clothes, don't spend money on any kind of entertainment. Pretend you don't have any money to spend.

You can take it further by learning how to live with less. Each time you want to make a purchase, ask yourself whether it's something you absolutely need. If not, chances are you'll regret the purchase and add more clutter to your life without any benefits. If you're not absolutely sure a purchase will bring long-term value in your life, have the discipline to skip it.

Exercise: Rejection Therapy

Rejection is an everyday part of our lives, yet most people can't handle it well. For many, it's so painful, they'd rather not ask for something at all than ask and risk rejection. Yet, as the old adage goes, if you don't ask, the answer is always no.

Avoiding rejection – which in essence means not having enough discipline to deal with this kind of discomfort – negatively affects many aspects of your life. All of that happens only because you're not tough enough to handle it.

For this reason, consider rejection therapy. Come up with a request or an activity that usually results in a rejection. Working in sales is one such example. Flirting with strangers is another. Haggling or asking for discounts at the stores will also work.

For more ideas, you can try the game of Rejection Therapy at http://rejectiontherapy.com/ where you can buy cards with various tasks designed to help you get rejected. 30 days of such a challenge is enough for a powerful shift that will not only help you become tougher, but also more self-confident.

By deliberately getting yourself rejected you'll grow a thicker skin that will allow you to take on much more in life, thus making you more successful at dealing with setbacks and unfavorable circumstances.

I performed a variation of this therapy when fighting my shyness. Getting repeatedly rejected made me feel okay with the feeling. After enough practice, my shyness was gone – you can't feel uncomfortable with things you do on a regular basis.

Exercise: Failure Therapy

Legendary baseball player and coach Yogi Berra once said, "Losing is a learning experience. It teaches you humility. It teaches you to work harder. It's also a powerful motivator."

Humility, work ethic, and motivation – all three of these are necessary components of personal growth and self-discipline.

If you're not humble, you'll overestimate your ability to resist temptations. In fact, a phenomenon called "restraint bias" shows that people overestimate their abilities to control impulses[xxxvii] and overexpose themselves to temptation.

Experiencing failure will keep you away from inflated impulse-control beliefs. You're not self-disciplined when you say you are – you're self-disciplined when you're smart enough to know how to avoid temptations altogether.

One of the best ways to get more familiar with failure in life is to strive to achieve difficult goals and set challenges that are potentially out of your reach. Just like a chess player can't keep improving his game playing against players worse than him, so you can't improve without constantly setting the bar higher.

The increased incidence of failure when setting difficult goals, and the subsequent feelings of discouragement, will be a worthwhile exercise to learn how to stay determined despite setbacks.

You don't challenge your self-discipline when you never experience failure. It's only when you make mistakes, jump through hoops, crawl under obstacles, and fall face forward when you can test and grow your determination.

Habit: Do the Most Difficult Things with No Hesitation

It's an old rule in the world of time management that you should do the most important things first, and only when you finish them are you allowed to move on to less essential activities.

However, few people follow this sound advice in everyday life. If you have a list of ten tasks to do, it's easier to focus on the easiest ones that you'd be able to cross off your list quickly.

It does nothing to move you closer to your goals (in fact, most of these quick tasks are probably unessential), yet you do it instead of the hard tasks. Why? Because it requires a lot of self-discipline to beat procrastination and get the uncomfortable tasks done first.

Change your habits and do the most difficult things first. Oftentimes, you can do what appears as a difficult and time-consuming task much more quickly than you think. It's only your perception of its difficulty that makes it so hard to get disciplined about it and get to work now.

As a writer, I have a simple routine of writing a certain number of words every single day. On the days I don't feel like writing, it's still one of the first things I do in the morning.

To break the reluctance, I simply write a few words and take it from there. A few minutes later, I no longer feel any resistance. The longer I hesitate, the weaker my resolve gets.

I find this to be the case with virtually every difficult activity I do. If I don't feel like working out in the morning, I don't sit and ponder whether I should go or not. I put on my fitness clothes and go. When I'm at the gym, I can't help but start – I've already taken the first step, and now things will only get easier.

Discomfort has a tendency to get overbearing the longer you let it simmer. If you don't give yourself a lot of time to think – instead opting to get the ball rolling and start working on the task – your reluctance will quickly melt away. Repeating the same process each time you don't feel like doing something will help you build a solid self-discipline-boosting habit.

Exercise: Learn Something Difficult

One of the most difficult but still manageable goals you can set for yourself to instill more discipline in your daily life is to learn a foreign language.

By making it a goal to become a fluent speaker in a language you don't speak, you'll not only acquire a valuable skill, but also discover how to learn in general. This also includes mastering how to deal with discouragement, which is always lurking somewhere nearby, ready to pounce the moment you struggle.

Learning foreign languages is a frustrating experience at every level, which means you'll get familiar with the feeling of frustration on a daily basis (and hopefully learn how to deal with it).

In the beginning, you'll experience frustration at not being able to understand anything. Later on, you'll get discouraged by what you will see as slow progress. Even when you're an advanced speaker, you'll still feel uncomfortable at times and get mad at yourself when you can't say something you know how to say perfectly in your native language.

These kinds of emotions are helpful to understand your patterns when learning a language or working on any difficult goal. What do you do when you feel like giving up? What leads you to this point? What snaps you out of it? Until you get started and experience these feelings on your own, you won't know the answers.

In my case, perfectionism is at the steering wheel of my discouragement. Each time I realize I'm far away from the perfect vision of my skills, I get frustrated. However, having discovered this pattern, I have turned it into an empowering one, using my anger as fuel to keep working on my abilities until they are as my mind pictures them.

What is it for you? How can you change your default response from the temptation to give up to more determination and discipline to keep going?

Here are several more difficult goals and skills to achieve that will help you elicit the same response and develop your own tactics to deal with discouragement and/or discomfort:

1. Learn a difficult sport requiring mastering proper technique

Some sports like basketball or football give a huge advantage to certain physical attributes, thus reducing the effectiveness of consistent practice. Few things are more frustrating than having an incredible work ethic and still being far behind other players with innate physical strengths. These sports won't help you build determination, and can only leave you bitter with the unfairness of the world.

To build more self-discipline by getting comfortable with difficulties, choose challenging sports that reward drills, consistent training, and going the extra mile.

Some of these sports include:

- golf

- chess

- tennis

- gymnastics

- wrestling or any martial arts that don't depend on your size

I'm not saying that you should become a world-class expert in any of these sports. The simple act of long-term practice, dealing with setbacks on the way toward progress, and achieving success is what you're after. The fact that it takes years to become at least average in these sports is what makes this exercise so powerful for building self-discipline.

In fact, a Canadian study has shown that regular, structured extracurricular sports seem to help kids develop self-discipline needed to engage effectively in the classroom. As professor Linda S. Pagani, one of the researchers said, "we found that those children who were specifically involved in team sports at kindergarten scored higher in self-regulation by time they reached fourth-grade"[xxxviii].

Not all is lost if you're an adult. You can start learning any sport you want at any age. The commitment needed to become an intermediate player in any of the more difficult sports will have the same effect on your self-discipline as in the case of kids.

2. Master a skill requiring patience

If you aren't patient enough to trust the process, you're more likely to give up too soon. If you expect quick results and don't achieve them, you'll be more likely to get discouraged and/or feel guilty you can't live up to your (unrealistic) expectations.

Here are some skills and activities that require a lot of patience, and thus the discipline to maintain focus and determination while waiting for the results:

- cooking, especially more difficult meals that require an hour or two of prep and one or two hours of cooking. Since cooking is a difficult skill to master (it takes dozens of tries to develop a "trademark" dish), it's perfect for exercising self-discipline.

- gardening. Most plants take months or years to grow. Some plants, like orchids, can live for months or years without sprouting a single flower. Talk about working on your patience.

- creative work. Painting, writing, and any other similar creative type of work requires a lot of determination and patience to see through to the very end. Even if it's something you're unlikely to show others, expressing yourself through art (and getting used to the long, arduous process of creation), will be helpful in developing more self-discipline.

- reading. You know how to read, you say? Well, when was the last time you finished an entire novel or full-length non-fiction work without skipping any part? Reading longer books requires patience and endurance – things that will help you grow more self-discipline.

- knitting. Firstly, learning how to knit takes months, if not years. Then, knitting an actual piece of clothing can take another few weeks, depending on what you want to knit and how complex it is. And how cool is it to be able to make your own clothes?

Now, don't get me wrong. The point is *not* to choose a difficult sport or skill you hate. If in the beginning something comes extremely hard to you and you don't enjoy it, there's a high chance you've already recognized subconsciously it's not a good activity for you.

For instance, I practiced judo for three months as a part of the curriculum at the university. I knew after the first few classes that it wasn't for me. I didn't enjoy it, I wasn't good at it, and it was extremely painful for my back. A few years later I started learning tennis. It only took me a few classes to realize I loved the sport, despite never before trying it.

3. Master honesty

According to a 2002 study at the University of Massachusetts, 60% of adults can't have a ten minute conversation without lying at least once (two to three times on average)[xxxix].

Granted, the study was conducted on 121 undergraduates, which is hardly a representation of the entire society. However, there are more sources that confirm the number of people lying regularly hovers around 50%.

According to Sunny Bates, CEO of New York-based executive recruitment firm Sunny Bates Associates, 40% of people lie on their résumés[xl].

According to online dating research from OkCupid, most of their users either lie about height (they are two inches shorter in real life) and income (people make 20% less than they say they are). They also lie about their pictures, stating they're recent while they were taken up to a few years ago.

It's not an understatement to say that lying is widespread and we encounter liars (or tell lies ourselves) every single day. It's difficult to remain honest, especially when what's at stake is your job, self-worth, or chances of meeting a life partner.

Yet mastering honesty is one of the best things you can do to improve the quality of your life and become comfortable with discomfort. After all, if telling the truth wasn't uncomfortable, nobody would lie.

A study conducted at the University of Notre Dame on 110 people between ages 18 and 71 has shown that telling fewer lies (including white lies) was linked with improved relationships (duh), fewer feelings of tension or melancholy (duh again, how can you not feel tense if you're lost in a web of lies?), and, what's most interesting, fewer health problems like headaches and sore throats[xli].

How do you stop lying if you're used to telling lies on a daily basis? Start with the realization that your lies – no matter if they're innocent white lies or more serious ones – hurt people. It affects your relationships by destroying trust, the basis of any human connection. Moreover, lies can follow you for years to come (lying on your résumé, lying to your partner), hurting you and those around you over and over again. All for a short-term gain – is it worth it?

Just like with any other activities that put you in discomfort, it takes time to become truly comfortable with being honest all the time. However, the regular practice of being upfront with people and the rewards you'll get for it will help you stay the course and join the minority of people who can be unconditionally trusted.

4. Learn communication skills

In essence, developing communication skills starts and ends with a habit of always putting yourself in the situation of the other person first. If you have enough discipline to tap into empathy before uttering a word, you'll become a better communicator and avoid conflicts.

However, it's not easy – and is certainly not comfortable – to resist the temptation to do the total opposite. It takes consistently applied discipline so you stick to your new ways rather than resorting to the old, ineffective communication patterns.

Negative communication habits, such as getting angry or fighting, are usually passing sensations that can be controlled if you make a conscious effort to catch them before giving in to them. By handling the impulse before making the situation worse, you'll master the ability to communicate with people without resorting to angry arguments.

The result of this practice – improved impulse control – will help you in other areas of life, teaching you how to trade a small instant reward with a larger, long-term, more positive result.

A lot of problems with communication also come from being too judgmental. It's easy to judge others without fully understanding their situation. It's an impulse similar to automatically arguing with someone instead of putting yourself in their shoes.

Learning how to handle this impulsive behavior is yet another exercise you can do to become more disciplined. The temptation to judge everyone and everything is often overpowering. It's easy to forget yourself and commence a long, useless tirade that serves nobody.

Try to catch yourself each time you find yourself judging someone else and stop. Saying bad things about others rarely helps anyone. Turn it into an empowering exercise by learning how to resist it.

Another negative communication habit to break is being unable or unwilling to state your needs and/or say no.

It's easier to relent and say that you'll do something rather than refuse and face the uncomfortable consequences of rejecting someone. That's why it's a good idea to learn how to voice your needs and put yourself in these uncomfortable situations so you can handle them better.

It can take years to see an improvement if you're naturally a person who puts other people first, but even then you can still feel bad about putting your needs over the needs of other people. However, it's a valuable and insightful practice that will help you deal better with awkward, uncomfortable situations that can arise when you say what you need or want (or when you say no and the other person doesn't take it well). You can't *not* grow your discipline by experiencing such circumstances frequently.

5. Learn to trust yourself

Obsessing over what other people think about you is nothing but the inability to have enough discipline to trust yourself. It's easier and more comfortable to ask for validation from other people than to learn how to feel okay without their approval.

It's equally easy to do what others tell you to do instead of sitting down and asking yourself what you truly want.

However, as we've already covered a few times in this book, choosing comfort rarely helps you achieve your goals. In the case of caring what others think about you or doing things to please them, you choose easy comfort (focusing on being liked) over discomfort that would bring more happiness (living your own life without concern about how others perceive you).

Obviously, not caring what others think has nothing to do with being insensitive or purposefully making yourself stand out. That would be another dimension of the same behavior – drawing your sense of self-worth from proving you *don't* need approval.

The sweet spot – requiring a lot of self-discipline to master – is to just *be the best version of yourself.* The opinion of others doesn't matter to you either way – it's neither about doing socially-accepted things nor going against the stream. It's about doing what's right to and for you and staying the course despite doubts and/or other people nagging you to change your path.

A personal example from my life comes from the two years spent at the university. Despite knowing well that college wouldn't be the right place for me, I relented because it was what young people after high school were supposed to do.

Two years later, I dropped out and decided to follow my own path, far away from the formal education and the 9 to 5 world. It was filled with doubt and difficulties, but in the end, carving my own path instead of following the prescribed route helped me reach my dream lifestyle. If it wasn't for the discipline to keep pushing despite not getting much approval from other people, I'm sure I wouldn't be so happy today.

In this case, the mental toughness I needed to travel my own path has helped me build the entire framework of my life and trust myself instead of choosing the easy way out by following what others do.

6. Stop complaining

For the majority of us, hardly a day goes by without uttering at least a few complaints.

I hate this weather. The traffic is so bad. She's always late. How dare he serve me cold dinner?

None of these complaints provide value in our lives, yet we continue to say them because it's easier than actually doing something about these things (or accepting them if we can't change them).

It's difficult and uncomfortable to stop complaining and instead turn toward solutions, but ultimately it's a powerful practice that will both help you grow as a person and become more in control of yourself.

Bestselling author and speaker Will Bowen suggests a 21-day complaint fast[xlii]. To complete the challenge, you can't complain for three weeks in a row. A slip up sends you back to day one, making it a difficult challenge that will require weeks or months to complete.

I used to complain endlessly, especially about the weather. When I reduced the number of my complaints (sometimes I still slip up) and accepted whatever I couldn't control, my life became happier and easier. This, in turn, helped me develop more self-discipline.

7. Overcome shyness

Few things can limit your chances of success more than shyness. A lack of confidence is a crippling condition that affects every single area of life, making it difficult to achieve goals and grow as a person.

It's also one of the most challenging problems to deal with, requiring incredible amounts of self-discipline to overcome. You can only deal with shyness by putting yourself in uncomfortable situations on a daily basis. The shier you are, the more stressful situations you have to experience before you become confident.

Months of constant exposure to stressors can test even the strongest people. However, the goal you'll ultimately achieve – a life free of being shy – is one of the most important goals you can ever accomplish.

I used to be a shy person for a large part of my life. It was my worst problem, but also one of the best things in my life because it forced me to travel the uncomfortable path to solve it.

Even if you don't suffer from terrible shyness (and merely don't consider yourself a particularly confident person), consider working on your self-confidence by exposing yourself to social circumstances you avoid (e.g., speaking with strangers).

Here are a few simple exercises to make you more comfortable with social awkwardness, which, in turn, will make you a more confident person:

- talk with random strangers. Chatting up random strangers is a powerful way to get rid of shyness. If you lack confidence, start with something simple and easy like asking for the directions or time (bonus points if you ask for the time with a phone in your hand or a watch on your wrist). If you have more courage, come up with weirder conversational topics or even flirt.

- practice eye contact. Initiate eye contact with strangers (or catch them gazing at you) and maintain it for as long as you can. Just don't forget to blink and keep a light smile. Otherwise you can make people uncomfortable, and that's not the point of this exercise. Bonus points for initiating eye contact, maintaining it and chatting up the person you're looking at.

- public speaking. If you're a shy person, few things are more awkward and difficult than standing in front of a group of people and presenting something with a trembling voice and shaky legs. However, that's exactly what you want to destroy your lack of confidence. I attended a few Toastmasters meetings in the past, and I found them an effective way to get used to speaking in front of strangers (as well as making new friends).

Obviously, these seven ideas present just a few different, challenging things you can work on to both experience immense personal growth and boost your self-discipline. The key is to find something that will force you to put yourself in uncomfortable situations to grow your comfort zone.

DISCOMFORT BUILDS CHARACTER: QUICK RECAP

1. By voluntarily putting yourself in uncomfortable situations you learn how to deal with adversity. Subsequently, you become tougher and more self-disciplined whenever you'll have to deal with new demanding situations.

2. Exposing yourself to cold temperatures can teach you how to deal with painful short-term situations. It will help you develop more awareness of your own responses and how you can keep going despite overpowering discomfort.

3. From time to time, try to do away with something you usually need – a certain habit or an item. It will help you appreciate it more while at the same time building your toughness (so in case such a situation happens out of your control, you'll be better able to handle it).

4. Rejection therapy – making it a goal to get rejected rather than accepted – is an effective way to get used to the mental discomfort of being told "no."

5. Exposing yourself to failure is a valuable exercise to stay humble and experience more learning opportunities. A large part of self-discipline is persistence. If you develop a habit to get up each time you fall, you'll have an easier time using your self-discipline in other situations that demand willpower.

6. Develop a habit to do the most difficult things with no hesitation. The longer you let yourself think before doing something that you find challenging, the more difficult it will be to gather enough willpower to do it. If you don't allow yourself to hesitate, soon you'll develop a habit that will make dealing with weakness easier.

7. Difficult goals require a great deal of mental toughness and self-discipline to achieve. If you constantly give yourself new difficult objectives to reach, you'll not only achieve more success in your life but also learn how to keep going despite setbacks and difficulties.

8. Learning a foreign language is one of the best self-discipline-building exercises because it's a long term goal (requiring at least six to twelve months of

your focus) and because it can cause a lot of frustrations tempting you to give up.

9. Other skills that require a lot of patience (and thus test your self-discipline and help you grow) include: sports requiring mastering proper technique like golf, tennis, or chess; cooking, gardening, creative work, reading, or knitting; and communication skills.

10. Challenging activities to help you grow as a person are a perfect way to develop more mental toughness and self-discipline. They usually require you to replace your default comfort-friendly choices with uncomfortable, but ultimately more beneficial, decisions. As a result, you'll improve your self-control. These goals and activities include: mastering honesty, trusting yourself, not complaining, and overcoming shyness.

Chapter 4: Live with Intent

The outer world follows your inner world. If there's chaos in your mind, there's chaos in your external world. If there's no peace in your head, everything around you can lead to stress.

If you have no discipline over your inner thoughts, you're unlikely to enjoy a lot of self-discipline in your everyday life.

Few people live their lives with intent. Everybody is too busy, too late, and too distracted to slow down and pay more attention to what is happening in their heads. Consequently, their inner life passes them by, influencing their outer world without them being conscious of it.

Building self-discipline is immensely more difficult if you only focus on the external aspect of it and disregard the power of your mind.

If you develop a calm mind capable of handling its thoughts – filtering useless ones, forming positive ones, and seeking justifications for doing the right things instead of coming up with excuses for not doing them – the act of self-control will become much easier.

How do you start living with more intent? It all starts with...

Habit: Sharpening Your Awareness with Quiet Repose

As famous management consultant Peter Drucker said, "What gets measured, gets managed." In the case of our thoughts, what gets observed, gets managed.

While it's impossible to manage all of our thoughts (according to various estimates, we have up to 70,000 thoughts a day[xliii]), we can pay attention to the ones that occur most frequently and control them – if we're only aware of them.

An average person doesn't pay a lot of attention to her thoughts. She assumes she is her thoughts and her feelings. If she *has a feeling* of anxiety, she *is* anxious. If she *thinks* she is stupid, she *is* stupid. If she *feels* she can't resist the temptation any longer, she *is not* self-disciplined. She associates herself with the fleeting thoughts that should report to her, and not the other way around.

How can you build permanent self-discipline if you give so much weight to your thoughts? Every doubt in your mind will ruin your resolve and solidify the belief that you can't become a more disciplined person.

The realization that you are not your thoughts and that they are passing sensations just like smells, sights, or sounds, will help you realize it's you who's in control of what you think. When you develop this ability, you'll gain the power to shape yourself as you wish.

The key to reaching this state of awareness is to regularly engage in the act of quiet repose. However, as much as I would like to encourage everyone to develop a regular habit of meditation, not all people enjoy it and find it worthwhile. Sitting still with your eyes closed can be too exhausting or just boring.

If you've tried it and didn't find it effective after doing it for at least a few weeks, here are a few alternatives worth testing.

1. Listen mindfully to music

And no, you're unlikely to have a meditative experience with heavy metal. Music most conducive to tuning down the world around you and exploring your inner world is instrumental or has soothing vocals harmonious with the rhythm of the song. Just like with meditation, the objective is to make the world around you disappear and reduce your being to the simple act of just being there (or in this case, just listening).

2. Practice yoga or tai chi

Yoga and tai chi are one of the few activities that get you as close to meditation as you can without actually meditating.

Maintaining a pose while focusing on your breath and letting go of the tension in your body is almost the description of meditation. The only difference is that you're not supposed to sit still, but engage in the meditative experience with your entire body.

Out of all the seven ideas listed here, it's the only type of a meditative experience that requires a teacher to perform properly (technically you can learn it from books and videos, but it's not an optimal way to go about it).

3. Journaling

The act of writing down your innermost thoughts can also be a meditative experience. It helps turn down the volume of the chatter in your mind and help you discover deeper layers of your inner world.

For best results, either journal by hand or do it on a computer without Internet access (or at least with email and social media notifications turned off). Otherwise, it's hard to fully immerse in the experience of projecting your thoughts onto a piece of paper (or screen).

4. Walking meditation

Walking meditation is originally known as *kinhin* in Buddhism. However, the practice of *kinhin* is more structured and requires walking clockwise around a room while taking steps synchronized with breath.

You don't have to follow this practice to a T – the mere act of mindful walking can be a meditative experience, too. For the best results, go to a park, a forest, or any other green place with as few distractions as possible. While walking, focus solely on the act of walking and your most immediate surroundings.

I used to do hill sprints a ten minute walk from my apartment. Each time I returned from my workout, my mind was filled with endorphins and naturally more prone to entering a meditative-like experience.

Oftentimes, lost in thought, I couldn't even remember a large part of my walk back home. That's precisely the feeling you're after – getting so lost in your inner world that you stop thinking about all of the distractions of the external world.

5. Gazing meditation

If you can't stand sitting still with your eyes closed, gazing meditation is an option for you. Known as *trāṭaka* in Hinduism, this method of meditation involves staring at a single point. It can be something as simple as a black dot on the wall, a tree in front of you or a candle flame (just don't gaze at the sun, okay?).

Just like any other type of meditation, gazing meditation is also effective at calming the restless mind. It also helps beginners maintain focus more effectively than sitting with eyes closed. Staring at a single point is more comfortable.

At times, I practice this type of meditation instead of the regular eyes-closed style. It's especially soothing when you're sitting in the wilderness and gaze at something beautiful (say, a flower in the middle of a meadow or an old tree and its rustling leaves).

6. Breathing meditation

While the traditional style of meditation is also about the focus on breathing, in this type of meditation you place all of your focus on breath.

There are various styles you can follow. Some prescribe long, slow inhales and quick exhales. Others recommend slow inhales, long pauses, and then slow exhales. No matter which breathing technique you use, the key is to shift all of your thoughts to the act of deep breathing.

Providing your body with more oxygen than usual (most people don't breathe deeply during the day) will have an additional effect of giving you more energy, so it's a good idea to practice this type of meditation in the morning.

7. Gratitude meditation

If the regular style of meditation is too boring for you because you can't stop having random thoughts constantly popping in your mind, consider replacing them with thoughts of gratitude.

If you occupy your mind with a certain type of thought (in this case, appreciation), other thoughts will stop appearing randomly (or at least stop occurring so frequently). This makes the act of maintaining inner focus and tuning out the world around you easier.

An additional advantage of this type of meditation is its mood-enhancing characteristic. You can't help but feel happier when you sit for five or ten minutes and come up with dozens or even hundreds of reasons why your life is incredible.

All of these meditative activities will help you become more aware of your inner thoughts. Once you become conscious of them, you can start living with more intent and control over your thoughts. You'll be able to shift them from negative to positive or observe them without judgment and let them go.

This practice, when repeated daily, builds self-control for your mind – you'll be more capable of dealing with nagging thoughts as well as impulsive emotions which always originate as a certain thought.

A craving for something is not hunger – it's a passing sensation that gets easier to overcome if you know that it passes just like any other thought. If you are aware of the thought of "This looks delicious" and can separate it from your actual state before it turns into the feeling of hunger, controlling your impulses will be much easier.

Try depersonalizing the craving by thinking "my body feels hunger" or "hunger is being felt." If you're the person observing the emotion, who's actually feeling it? Most certainly not you – and that's a helpful mind-bending trick to handle temptations better.

The same applies to thoughts of defeat or discouragement – just like the feeling of a craving, they are passing. True, they can linger for more than a few minutes, but they also pass – just like the random thoughts appearing in your mind as you meditate. By simply being aware of this fact, you can grow your ability to wait on these feelings before they urge you to take the (wrong) action.

Please keep in mind, I'm by no means a meditation expert. Some of the types of meditative practices I mentioned before have fluid definitions and can be used interchangeably or at the same time. For instance, you can combine walking meditation with gratitude meditation or combine yoga and listening with intent to calming music.

A special alternative, or rather, a supplemental activity in addition to some type of a meditative practice is...

Exercise: Embracing the Tunnel Vision

Meditation is not only something done as a specific activity at a specific time. You can also practice it on a daily basis to become more in control over distractions. Each time you slow down, become mindful of what you do, and focus on the sensation a specific experience gives you, you gain more control over your mind.

Each day, we miss hundreds, if not thousands, of special experiences just because we're distracted by other things. Oftentimes, these distractions lead us to give in to temptations, sometimes unconsciously.

You're late for a meeting, so you grab the first piece of food you can reach (usually something unhealthy) and go on your way. If you slowed down and cleared your mind of the distracting thoughts, temptations would be much less challenging to overcome.

Embracing the tunnel vision can help with this. The first component of this exercise is to be able to slow down. You can't do it well if you're in a hurry. If you can set aside at least a few minutes (or just utilize breaks between your activities) when you can truly focus on the present moment without worrying about what you're about to do, you can proceed to the second step – becoming mindful.

As an example, let's say you're out in the woods enjoying a brief walk. While being in nature alone is conducive to fewer distractions, there's something more you can do to enter a meditative-like state and clear your mind.

Pick up a leaf, touch the bark of a tree, or look at a bird or a squirrel. Engage all of your senses; let yourself be swallowed by the experience of it. Trace the contours of the leaf. Feel its texture. Gaze at its intense color. Smell it.

Use your willpower to focus all of your attention on the leaf in your palm. Tune out the world around you. Let yourself feel all these weird sensations of getting intimate with a leaf. In the beginning, you probably won't be able to do it longer than a few seconds. After all, who in their right mind spends a minute or two staring at a simple leaf (and for that matter, who the heck with a sane mind talks about "getting intimate" with a leaf?).

However, the disciplined practice of seeing the little details everybody else ignores not only makes the world a much more interesting place, but also sharpens your awareness. As a result, you become more equipped to identify and deal with temptations before they become overbearing.

The problem with many self-defeating feelings and thoughts is not only that they arise. It's that you aren't aware of them and let them dictate your behavior without paying much attention to it.

Our minds are incredible at justifying every single action we take. It's only in retrospect when we can say that our decisions were stupid and dictated by how we felt at a specific moment (and it doesn't sound like healthy decision making, does it?).

A short attention span is what causes this problem. By embracing the tunnel vision regularly, you'll improve your ability to focus and thus reduce the risk of making emotionally-motivated decisions.

Exercise: Talk with Your Future Self

Each time you choose a smaller reward now instead of a larger reward later, you're robbing your future self. We're bad at envisioning our future selves and associating who we are now with the person we'll be in a year.

This person sounds like a stranger, not like us. And since it's a stranger, it's easier to claim small rewards now than to wait for better rewards later. After all, we're here now, not in the future, right?

In psychology, there's a concept called temporal discounting[xliv] – the tendency to give greater value to rewards received now or soon in comparison to the rewards received later in the future. You prefer $100 now over $200 in a year or a free pizza in 2 hours over two free pizzas in 6 months.

When applied to self-discipline, due to the temporal discounting, you'll give more value to satisfying your craving now than achieving your ideal physique in 6 months. After all, the first reward is real, at your fingertips, and the second reward (and the vision of you in 6 months) is just a concept, something difficult to imagine.

The exercise I'm about to describe is meant to solve this problem. We have problems imagining ourselves in the future because we rarely do it. You can solve the problem of the disassociation between your present self and your future self by writing a letter to your present self from the perspective of your future self.

Let's say you'd like to lose twenty pounds and get fit. However, you struggle with this goal because you can't give more value to the future reward (healthy physique) over the instant reward (eating food you love). Consequently, instant gratification always wins.

Now imagine yourself in the future as a person who hasn't achieved this goal, who decided to rob his or her future self. Make the picture even worse than your current situation – you weigh even more than now, and your weight keeps going up.

What would your future (obese) self say? Would he or she be happy that you've chosen caving in to a temptation over achieving the long term goal? How does the perspective of an even worse future affect your self-discipline today?

If you imagine every single detail and make it an emotional process of visualization, chances are your future self will cease being a virtual concept and become something real.

You can also try the opposite by imagining your future self as a person who has achieved the goal of losing weight. What would your future (fit) self say about sticking to your goal? How would the path toward the objective look to a person who has already achieved it?

It's often easier to imagine reaching the goal (and the person you'll become) if you visualize the perfect result and then trace back every single step needed to accomplish it (vs figuring it out from where you are now).

Exercise: Build Your Compass

How aware are you of your most important values and priorities in life? How do they affect your decision making process?

When asked, most people wouldn't hesitate to say their most important values include health, family, or freedom. Yet, their daily lives don't reflect it because they don't have clear rules regarding their values – a personal compass to guide them.

Every several months, make a list of your most important values and ask yourself whether your everyday actions follow them. One of the most powerful forces is the need for integrity. If you uncover that health is of utmost importance to you, but recently you've gained a few pounds and stopped exercising as often as before, it can give you a kick needed to get back on track.

Living with intent requires a clear mind and focus. Having a set of clearly-defined values (and the following habits or rules you need to practice to be consistent with them) will help you maintain a steady level of self-discipline in life.

LIVE WITH INTENT: QUICK RECAP

1. A calm, focused mind is a powerful tool that will help you resist temptations and reach your goals despite setbacks, failures, and distractions. Living with intent is a must if you'd like to become a person with a lot of self-control.

2. Living with intent starts with sharpening your awareness. The easiest way to become more focused and present instead of distracted and mindless is to engage in a meditative practice. The act of focusing on the inner world and quieting the external world around you is one of the keys to a calm, disciplined mind.

3. In addition to regular meditation, there are at least seven alternatives. You can try each to see which is most effective at helping you calm the chatter in your head. You can listen mindfully to music, practice yoga or tai chi, try journaling, or experiment with walking, gazing, breathing, or gratitude meditation. You can even try a mixture.

4. Without the ability to see the little things and use all of your senses while doing so, discovering

what makes you prone to give in to temptation will be more difficult. Embracing the tunnel vision – exercising your focus on a single thing to experience it with all your senses – is helpful to improve your attention span and prevent making emotional decisions.

5. Due to temporal discounting, people are prone to give greater value to rewards they can get soon (in hours) than the rewards they'll get in the future (in weeks or months), even if the future rewards are bigger. Imagining your future self can make the prospect of future easier to grasp. As a result, you'll stop robbing the person you'll become of rewards just because you give more value to your current self (even if the reward is much smaller and not beneficial for you long term).

6. Have a compass of your personal values. Without a clearly defined set of priorities in life, it's easy to stray off the course and do things that don't reflect what you believe in. Periodically reminding yourself of what's most important to you can help

you make changes to regain self-control and fix the crucial things you've neglected.

Chapter 5: Burnout and Discouragement – It's Not All About Self-Discipline

It was one of those days when I felt too exhausted to go to the gym, but went anyway. After a demanding workout, I got back home with legs that felt like huge stones and a tense, aching back.

I called a friend and we went to a sauna. I thought it would be a great way to relax my body and recover from my workout.

Not this time.

After spending ten minutes in a dry sauna, I submerged for a few minutes in a pool of ice cold water, as I usually do. I could feel something was wrong almost right away. My vision blurred and I became dizzy.

I ignored these symptoms. I thought they would pass in a second.

But they didn't. A couple of minutes later, I realized that if I didn't leave the pool right away, I would faint. I climbed the pool ladder out with the world spinning around me.

Leaning against the wall, I barely made a few shaky steps before I had to sit down on the floor so I wouldn't fall.

For ten minutes I fought with intense vertigo and nausea. I finally resigned, asking my friend to call the lifeguard for assistance. It took me about an hour of cooling my neck (lifeguard's prescription) and suffering the worst feeling of dizziness in my life before I could go to the locker room. It took me another thirty minutes of sitting in the car before I was ready to drive, and another few hours of sleep at home before I finally felt well again.

The next day I woke up with a sore throat, painful joints, and full-body exhaustion. I was sick for a few days, unable to do anything productive, let alone go to the gym. It would be a few months before I would be brave enough to go to the sauna again. To this day, I don't feel entirely comfortable staying in a dry sauna for longer than a few minutes.

I have since learned my lesson that nobody is indestructible. My obsession with self-discipline went too far. I not only ignored the first signal (by going to the gym), but the second one as well (not immediately leaving the ice cold pool when something felt wrong).

Now I pay more attention to my body and give myself regular breaks from workouts and no longer play too aggressively with extreme temperatures. I still challenge myself, but do so in a safer way to avoid overextending myself.

If you're anything like me, you may feel tempted to think you can withstand much more than a regular person. But as much as being mentally tough is helpful, it doesn't mean you should cross all the limits and do things that endanger your health or your life.

Stretch Yourself, but Don't Break Yourself

Deliberately putting yourself into uncomfortable situations is helpful, but don't forget it shouldn't become unbearable. Every exercise in this book is meant to be practiced often, but not when your body is giving you obvious signals it can't take more.

The same applies to your mental strength. While willpower probably depends on whether we believe it's limited or not[xlv] (and not, like Kelly McGonigal[xlvi] and Roy Bauimester[xlvii] say, depends on your glucose levels), there's a point when discomfort becomes too much to handle. The sweet spot is to stretch your comfort zone to such an extent that you feel challenged, but not too threatened or frustrated.

Going past the bearable level of discomfort can result in diminished effectiveness, and often in negative outcomes that actually work against you.

Hardcore workaholics are proud to work 70+ hours a week, thinking they're so extremely self-disciplined and tough everybody should clap their hands when they see them. In fact, what they do is the total opposite of smart. Research has proven that someone who works 70 hours produces nothing more with those extra 15 hours than a person working 55 hours a week[xlviii].

I used to follow a routine of writing 3,000 words every single day. I stuck to it for a couple of months, feeling proud of myself and my ability to write so much every single day. Then one day my entire willpower was gone, replaced by frustration and overwhelming reluctance. Even writing a single sentence was too much. My routine became too demanding, and nothing but taking a long break could help me get back to writing.

If I started with writing 1,000 words a day and then gradually increased my word count until it felt challenging, but still not too demanding, I would probably have never experienced such a burnout.

True, I would only write up to 1,500 words or so a day, but my routine would be more sustainable, and thus more effective long-term.

Self-discipline isn't built overnight. If you want to become mentally tougher and more in control over your temptations, play the long game and prioritize sustainability over quick results.

If you want to introduce more discomfort in your life for the purpose of becoming tougher and more disciplined, remember that it's not about putting too much stress on yourself for the short term. It's about desensitizing – gradual and repeated exposure to a stressor.

Without proper rest, you won't master new skills quickly, recover enough to have another workout, or stick to your routine for more than a few months.

Each time you set a new daily routine or a goal you'd like to achieve, don't forget to schedule break times. It can be one or two days a week when you don't practice at all, regular cheat days to have a psychological break from the diet, a day or two of guilt-free laziness when working on a business, or two weeks of vacation each year.

Positive Mindset Is Essential for Mental Toughness (and Vice Versa)

The essence of building self-discipline and mental toughness is making your life harder so you can better handle temptations, setbacks, and failures in life.

In addition to making you tougher, these exercises can help you appreciate what you have more. Consequently, you become a more grateful person with a positive mindset that will support you on a daily basis.

If you start a 30-day cold shower challenge, a month from now you'll gain a newfound appreciation for the 24/7 availability of hot showers. If you start learning a foreign language, you'll become more appreciative of the fact you already speak the most important language in the world. If you skip food for 24-48 hours, you'll gain more gratitude for the fact there's always food in your fridge (and you'll enjoy its taste more, too).

As I've already covered it in my book, *Pure and Simple: How to Simplify Your Life, Do Less, and Get More*, gratitude is one of the keys to have a positive mindset. It improves mental and physical health, helps make friends, reduces aggression, increases empathy, and alleviates stress and trauma.

Working on your self-discipline and mental toughness will help you become a more successful person. However, it's your ability to appreciate what you have and keep a positive outlook that will help you get back on track after a particularly defeating failure or setback.

If self-discipline is the only reason why you keep going, one day you can find yourself depleted of your willpower. The second layer of motivation – a positive mindset – will keep you going when you don't feel like doing anything and all willpower is gone.

"Easy" temptations like not eating a cake during a diet, not wanting to put on jogging shoes, or clicking the snooze button instead of waking up early can be dealt with using self-discipline alone. Train your willpower, develop better default responses and you can overcome the majority of these temptations.

Hard, unexpected temptations and problems challenging your resolve can wreak havoc on your self-discipline.

If you've lost a business, willpower and toughness alone might not be enough to get back on track and start another business within days after the failure.

Tough, self-disciplined people may feel tempted to blame themselves for everything that has happened to them. Or worse yet – they may find themselves tempted to keep working on the business, thinking that giving up (when it would make sense to do so) would be a sign of a weakness.

People who can appreciate what they still have (for instance, a supporting wife or the learning experience) have something more useful in such a situation than mere self-discipline – psychological resilience and the ability to move on. If something fails, it fails. Learn the lessons and keep going.

Focusing on the positive emotion (gratitude) instead of the negative one (guilt) is what will help you avoid the long spiral down. There's a world of difference between a person who cheats and then blames herself for being weak-minded and a person who tells herself "it's fine to slip up every now and then, now it's just time to hop back on the train."

The first person will keep blaming herself, possibly for so long and so severely she'll realize it makes no sense to continue working on whatever goal she had been working on. The second person – while technically experiencing the same setback as the first person – will not make it worse by letting herself feel guilty. She'll pick up where she left off and keep moving forward.

Just like I shouldn't have gone to the gym when I felt clear signs of overtraining, you shouldn't always demand perfect toughness and self-discipline from yourself. Move with the wind, don't resist it.

How Focusing on Negativity Can Ruin Your Self-Discipline

We're naturally wired to focus more on negativity than positivity. In psychology, it's called the negativity bias[xlix]. Something very positive has a smaller impact on your behavior than something of equal emotional strength, but negative.

It's a Monday morning, the fifth week of Alice's diet. She steps on the scales and sees that her weight has gone down by another pound. She's happy and grateful, but she quickly forgets about it because she's been steadily losing her weight for the last five weeks.

Another week has passed. She looks at the number and freezes. Instead of losing another pound, she has gained a pound.

A pound more should carry the same emotional load (albeit negative) than losing a pound a week ago. Yet, now her behavior is completely different.

She doesn't forget about it right after stepping off the scales. She keeps thinking about it for the entire day, if not the entire week.

She thinks she messed something up, or maybe her diet just no longer works and it's better to give up than experience yet another letdown next week.

Can you see how easy it is to destroy your entire progress by putting too much focus on negativity?

Fortunately, a process called cognitive reappraisal[1] – reinterpreting the meaning of the negative event to give it a positive slant – can help handle this problem.

In Alice's case, we can reinterpret it in a few different ways.

She can either reinterpret it as gaining a pound of water, thus making it a short-term problem. Then it wouldn't be a sign of her diet losing its effectiveness, just a temporary condition, which should prevent any emotional behaviors from happening.

She can reinterpret it as gaining a pound of muscle. In some people, it's possible to burn fat and gain muscle at the same time, and that is even better for Alice's physique than only losing a pound of fat.

She can also reinterpret it as an opportunity to take a closer look at her diet and make sure she's been faithful to her resolutions. Perhaps she slipped up and didn't notice it? A pound gained this week can help her reverse the trend before it gets worse.

You can use cognitive reappraisal for every similar situation to change its meaning and stop yourself from falling into despair.

What to Do When You're Stuck in a Funk or Suffer from Negative Self-Talk

When working on self-discipline, it's easy to go from one extreme (a lack of self-discipline) to another (being too tough on yourself). Now that you're working on your discipline, you tend to get tougher on yourself and criticize yourself even more often and more heavily than before.

Soon, negative self-talk follows, berating you for every single failure or even a temptation (including the ones you were able to overcome). It's clear to see it's not an optimal way to build long-term self-discipline.

How do you deal with this problem and empower yourself with your thoughts instead of bringing out your inner critic? Start with developing more self-compassion.

In her book "The Charisma Myth: How Anyone Can Master the Art and Science of Personal Magnetism" Olivia Fox Cabane says that the higher one's level of self-compassion, the lower one's level of self-pity[li]. Self-pity brings out all of those pesky negative thoughts and hinders our progress.

There are several ways to build more self-compassion and consequently get out of a funk or escape negative self-talk.

My favorite one – and also the simplest one – is to make a list of ways to boost your mood that make you feel you care about yourself. Each time you feel stuck or berate yourself for how stupid, weak, unworthy, or untalented you are, check your list and get your energy levels up.

I have 31 such things on my list I titled "Ways to Go from Pain to Pleasure and Feel Good Immediately." To give you a few examples, the list contains things as simple as listening to a specific genre of music (including specific tracks), sitting in the sun, or talking with friends as well as more creative ways such as giving someone a gift, telling someone I appreciate her, or coming up with new ideas.

Make your own list. Read it each time you feel down and pick a thing or two to boost your mood. It's difficult to come up with ways to lift your spirits if you feel discouraged or frustrated. Having a ready list of proven ways to get better is helpful to remind yourself there are things you can do to feel better, and it's your choice to remain in an unproductive state of mind.

You can also get out of a funk by influencing your body language instead of your mind. If you stand upright, light up your face with a wide smile (it doesn't matter if it's fake), and start jumping up and down while waving your hands, it's virtually impossible to stay depressed.

Science supports this wild advice. A study conducted on power posing has shown that assuming a high-power body language causes neuroendocrine and behavioral changes[lii]. It elevates testosterone, decreases cortisol, and increases feelings of power and tolerance for risk. Assuming a power pose for just a minute or two is enough to make you feel more powerful – and not just have a fake feeling of power.

If you suffer from negative self-talk due to being tougher on yourself than on other people, a simple visualization technique can also help. Instead of looking at yourself through your own eyes, imagine you're a friend, family member, or anyone else who loves you.

How does your perception of yourself change when you look at yourself through the eyes of someone who loves you? A simple realization that you wouldn't treat others you love as you treat yourself can help you eliminate, or at least reduce the negative self-talk.

Don't forget that negative self-talk doesn't necessarily have to come from your inner critic. It can also be a result of a tired body – when you've over trained, have been following a strict diet for too long, or haven't slept well for the past week.

If your body is tired, it's easy to get into a cranky mood and start doubting yourself or thinking that you can't bear anything for much longer. Check your physical state and make sure you get enough sleep, nutrients (dieting can sometimes cause deficiencies), sun (a lack of vitamin D the body synthesizes with sun exposure can possibly cause depression[liii]), and quiet time (a hectic schedule can elevate your stress levels).

BURNOUT AND DISCOURAGEMENT – IT'S NOT ALL ABOUT SELF-DISCIPLINE: QUICK RECAP

1. Discomfort is not always a good idea. If your body is screaming to take care of it, don't put it into new stressful situations. Develop a keen sense of your energy levels as well as your general wellbeing. The point of the exercises in this book isn't to endanger your health or turn your life into a nightmare.

2. While growth rarely (if ever) happens if you constantly avoid discomfort, there's a fine line between beneficial and empowering discomfort and the panic zone when things get too stressful. If you put too much on your shoulders and expect to perform well in the long term, you're in for a nasty surprise.

3. A positive mindset is a necessary part of a personality needed to become a self-disciplined, relentless person. Sometimes your willpower won't be enough to keep going after a particularly devastating blow, or simply the act of constantly being tough will exhaust you. In these cases, a

positive outlook can help you get back on track by redirecting your focus from the failure to the appreciation of what you have.

4. Guilt is never a good emotion for a person building self-discipline. It increases the likelihood of making your slip-up even more severe by thinking that the failure is worse than it actually is. Not resisting the temptation to eat a candy bar is not the end of your diet as long as you don't follow it with guilt-motivated why-the-hell-not-I-already-failed binge eating.

5. Due to the negativity bias, we focus more on negative events than the positive ones (even if they carry the same emotional weight). You can use cognitive reappraisal to reinterpret the meaning of the bad event and turn it into a positive one. Thanks to this process, you'll avoid the discouragement that can increase the chances of losing your willpower.

6. You can deal with negative self-talk and/or get out of a funk by developing more self-compassion. Some of the most effective strategies include making a list of ways to pamper yourself, changing your body

language to mimic the appearance of a happy person, or looking at yourself from the perspective of someone else. A negative mindset is often also the result of sleep deficiencies, a deficiency of certain nutrients (including vitamin D), or going too long with a strict diet or a workout schedule.

Epilogue

We've covered a lot of habits, exercises, and mindset shifts that will help you become a more self-disciplined person. However, it doesn't mean you should start changing every single aspect of your life right away. For the best results, pick one or two things you'd like to improve and proceed from there once you make the changes and become more disciplined.

If you aren't fit yet, working on your health and fitness should become your priority. There's no other goal that is more important than developing proper healthy habits. Without a healthy body, nothing else matters.

Moving from an unhealthy and overweight person to a fit, vibrant individual is one of the best changes you can undergo to develop your general discipline. With renewed energy levels and a heightened sense of well-being, all other challenges will be much easier and more enjoyable to achieve.

Learning how to be consistent and stay the course is the most powerful secret behind mental toughness and self-discipline. If you adhere to your routine and reach a long-term goal in one aspect of your life, achieving the same in other areas will be easier. Success tends to breed success, but first you have to experience some small wins – and they are the most crucial in the health and fitness department.

If you're already a fit person, feel free to pick any other habit or exercise. Ideally, choose something related to your long-term goals.

If you find yourself giving up when working on difficult goals (or if you have a tendency to jump from one thing to another without ever mastering anything), choose a difficult skill or sport to master and dedicate yourself to the process of learning. Use it as a tool for self-introspection and building your own arsenal of weapons to deal with self-defeating thoughts and behaviors.

Everything valuable in life requires time and dedication. The world wants you to prove you care about whatever you're chasing after. Only the ones who can maintain discipline, motivation, determination, and commitment over the long term will enjoy the reward of achieving their goals. If you exhibit this kind of an attitude and constantly remind yourself of it, I'm sure you'll push through all the obstacles and get wherever you want to get.

Download another Book for Free

I want to thank you for buying my book and offer you another book (just as valuable as this book), *Grit: How to Keep Going When You Want to Give Up*, completely free.

Visit the link below to receive it:

http://www.profoundselfimprovement.com/dailyselfdiscipline

In *Grit*, I'll share with you exactly how to stick to your goals according to peak performers and science.

In addition to getting *Grit*, you'll also have an opportunity to get my new books for free, enter giveaways, and receive other valuable emails from me.

Again, here's the link to sign up:

http://www.profoundselfimprovement.com/dailyselfdiscipline

Could You Help?

I'd love to hear your opinion about my book. In the world of book publishing, there are few things more valuable than honest reviews from a wide variety of readers.

Your review will help other readers find out whether my book is for them. It will also help me reach more readers by increasing the visibility of my book.

About Martin Meadows

Martin Meadows is the pen name of an author who has dedicated his life to personal growth. He constantly reinvents himself by making drastic changes in his life.

Over the years, he has regularly fasted for over 40 hours, taught himself two foreign languages, lost over 30 pounds in 12 weeks, ran several businesses in various industries, took ice-cold showers and baths, lived on a small tropical island in a foreign country for several months, and wrote a 400-page long novel's worth of short stories in one month.

Yet, self-torture is not his passion. Martin likes to test his boundaries to discover how far his comfort zone goes.

His findings (based both on his personal experience and scientific studies) help him improve his life. If you're interested in pushing your limits and learning how to become the best version of yourself, you'll love Martin's works.

You can read his books here:

http://www.amazon.com/author/martinmeadows.

[i] Wing R. R., Phelan S., "Long-term weight loss maintenance." *The American Journal of Clinical Nutrition* 2005; 82 (1): 222–225.

[ii] http://fourhourworkweek.com/2012/07/12/how-to-lose-100-pounds/, Web., September 10th, 2015. For more information, read Ferriss T., *The 4-Hour Body: An Uncommon Guide to Rapid Fat Loss, Incredible Sex and Becoming Superhuman*, 2010.

[iii] Keyes R., *The Quote Verifier: Who Said What, Where, and When*, 2006, p. 160.

[iv] http://quod.lib.umich.edu/l/lincoln/, Web. September 25th, 2015.

[v] Ogden C. L., Carroll M. D., Kit B. K., Flegal K. M., "Prevalence of Childhood and Adult Obesity in the United States, 2011–2012." *The Journal of the American Medical Association* 2014; 311 (8): 806–814.

[vi] Duhigg C., *The Power of Habit: Why We Do What We Do in Life and Business*, 2012.

[vii] Blair S. N., Jacobs D. R., Jr., Powell K. E., "Relationships between exercise or physical activity and other health behaviors." *Public Health Reports* 1985; 100 (2): 172–180.

[viii] DeMarco MJ, *The Millionaire Fastlane: Crack the Code to Wealth and Live Rich for a Lifetime*, 2011.

[ix] Rhodes R. E., de Bruijn G. J., "How big is the physical activity intention-behaviour gap? A meta-analysis using the action control framework." *British Journal of Health Psychology* 2013; 18 (2): 296–309.

[x] http://www.statisticbrain.com/gym-membership-statistics/, Web., September 9th, 2015.

[xi] Medbo J. I., Mohn A. C., Tabata I, Bahr R, Vaage O, Sejersted O. M., "Anaerobic capacity determined by maximal accumulated O2 deficit." *Journal of Applied Physiology* 1988; 64 (1): 50–60.

[xii] A good introduction to hill sprints can be found here: http://jasonferruggia.com/hill-sprints-for-fat-loss/.

[xiii] Petruzzello S. J., Landers D. M., Hatfield B. D., Kubitz K. A., Salazar W., "A Meta-Analysis on the Anxiety-Reducing Effects of Acute and Chronic Exercise." *Sports Medicine* 1991; 11 (3): 143–182.

[xiv] Raichlen D. A., Foster A. D., Gerdeman G. L., Seillier A., Giuffrida A., "Wired to run: exercise-induced endocannabinoid signaling in humans and cursorial mammals with implications for the 'runner's high'." *The Journal of Experimental Biology* 2012; 215 (8): 1331–1336.

[xv] Coon D., Mitterer J. O., *Introduction to Psychology: Gateways to Mind and Behavior*, 2012.

[xvi] Karageorghis C. I., Terry P. C., *Inside Sport Psychology*, 1969.

[xvii] Ryan R. M., Frederick C. M., Lepes D., Rubio N., Sheldon K. M., "Intrinsic Motivation and Exercise Adherence." *International Journal of Sport Psychology* 1997; 28: 335–354.

[xviii] A workout consisting of squat, deadlifts and bench presses is superior to using machines. Learn more here: http://rippedbody.jp/the-big-3-routine/.

[xix] Irwin B. C., Scorniaenchi J., Kerr N. L., Eisenmann J. C., Feltz D. L., "Aerobic exercise is promoted when individual performance affects the group: a test of the Kohler motivation gain effect." *Annals of Behavioral Medicine: a Publication of the Society of Behavioral Medicine* 2012; 44 (2): 151–9.

[xx] Feltz D. L., Irwin B. C., Kerr N., "Two-player partnered exergame for obesity prevention: using discrepancy in players' abilities as a strategy to motivate physical activity." *Journal of Diabetes Science and Technology* 2012; 6 (4): 820–7.

[xxi] Osborn K. A., Irwin B. C., Skogsberg N. J., Feltz D. L., "The Köhler effect: Motivation gains and losses in real sports groups." *Sport, Exercise, and Performance Psychology* 2012; 1 (4): 242–253.

[xxii] Polivy J., Herman C. P., "If at first you don't succeed: False hopes of self-change." *American Psychologist* 2002; 57 (9): 677–689.

[xxiii] http://www.marksdailyapple.com/exercising-when-sick, Web. September 12th, 2015.

[xxiv] Ogasawara R., Yasuda T., Sakamaki M., Ozaki h., Abe T., "Effects of periodic and continued resistance training on muscle CSA and strength in previously untrained men." *Clinical Physiology and Functional Imaging* 2011; 31 (5): 399–404.

[xxv] https://www.youtube.com/watch?v=e1Vriq2ORZI, Web., September 14th, 2015.

[xxvi] Katz D. L, Meller S., "Can We Say What Diet Is Best for Health?" *Annual Review of Public Health* 2014; 35: 83–103.

[xxvii] Mischel W., Ebbesen E. B., Raskoff Z. A., "Cognitive and attentional mechanisms in delay of gratification." *Journal of Personality and Social Psychology* 1972; 21 (2): 204–218.

[xxviii] Shoda Y., Mischel W. Peake P. K., "Predicting Adolescent Cognitive and Self-Regulatory Competencies from Preschool Delay of Gratification: Identifying Diagnostic Conditions." *Developmental Psychology* 1990; 26 (6): 978–986.

[xxix] Loewenstein G., "Hot-cold empathy gaps and medical decision making." *Health Psychology* 2005; 24 (4): S49–S56.

[xxx] Ariely D., Loewenstein G., "The heat of the moment: the effect of sexual arousal on sexual decision making." *Journal of Behavioral Decision Making* 2006; 19: 87–98.

[xxxi] Dirlewanger M., di Vetta V., Guenat E., Battilana P., Seematter G., Schneiter P., Jéquier E., Tappy L., "Effects of short-term carbohydrate or fat overfeeding on energy expenditure and plasma leptin concentrations in healthy female subjects." *International Journal of Obesity and Related Metabolic Disorders: Journal of the International Association for the Study of Obesity* 2000; 24 (11): 1413–8.

[xxxii] Davis J. F., "Adipostatic regulation of motivation and emotion." *Discovery Medicine* 2010; 9 (48): 462–7.

[xxxiii] A study about the need to have a high-protein cheat day: Bray G. A., Smith S. R., de Jonge L., Xie H., Rood J., Martin C. K., Most M., Brock C., Mancuso S., Redman L. M., "Effect of dietary protein content on weight gain, energy expenditure, and body composition during overeating: a randomized controlled

146

trial." *JAMA* 2012; 307 (1): 47–55. A study about high-carb refeeding: Dirlewanger M., di Vetta V., Guenat E., Battilana P., Seematter G., Schneiter P., Jéquier E., Tappy L., "Effects of short-term carbohydrate or fat overfeeding on energy expenditure and plasma leptin concentrations in healthy female subjects." *International Journal of Obesity and Related Metabolic Disorders: Journal of the International Association for the Study of Obesity* 2000; 24 (11): 1413–8.

[xxxiv] You can also refer to this article for scientific explanations: http://www.leangains.com/2010/10/top-ten-fasting-myths-debunked.html.

[xxxv] Rosenberg J., Maximov I. I., Reske M., Grinberg F., Shah N. J., "Early to bed, early to rise": Diffusion tensor imaging identifies chronotype-specificity." *NeuroImage* 2014; 84 (1): 428–434.

[xxxvi] Irwine W. B., *A Guide to the Good Life: The Ancient Art of Stoic Joy*, 2008.

[xxxvii] Nordgren L. F., van Harreveld F., van der Pligt J., "The restraint bias: how the illusion of self-restraint promotes impulsive behavior." *Psychological Science* 2009; 20 (12): 1523–8.

[xxxviii] Piché G., Fitzpatrick C., Pagani L. S., "Associations Between Extracurricular Activity and Self-Regulation: A Longitudinal Study From 5 to 10 Years of Age." *American Journal of Health Promotion* 2014, 30 (1): 32–40.

[xxxix] Feldman R. S., Forrest J. A., Happ B. R., "Self-Presentation and Verbal Deception: Do Self-Presenters Lie More?" *Basic and Applied Social Psychology* 2002; 24 (2): 163–170.

[xl] http://www.forbes.com/2006/05/20/resume-lies-work_cx_kdt_06work_0523lies.html, Web., September 29th, 2015.

[xli] http://www.apa.org/news/press/releases/2012/08/lying-less.aspx, Web., September 29th, 2015.

[xlii] Bowen W., *A Complaint Free World: How to Stop Complaining and Start Enjoying the Life You Always Wanted*, 2013.

http://blogs.discovermagazine.com/neuroskeptic/2012/05/09/the-70000-thoughts-per-day-myth/, Web., October 2nd, 2015.

[xliv] Doyle J. R., "Survey of time preference, delay discounting models." *Judgment and Decision Making* 2013; 8 (2): 116–135.

[xlv] Miller E. M., Walton G. M., Dweck C. S., Job V., Trzesniewski K., McClure S. M. "Theories of Willpower Affect Sustained Learning." *PLoS ONE* 2012, 7 (6).

[xlvi] McGonigal K., *The Willpower Instinct: How Self-Control Works, Why It Matters, and What You Can Do to Get More of It*, 2013.

[xlvii] Baumeister R. F., Tierney J., *Willpower: Rediscovering the Greatest Human Strength*, 2012.

[xlviii] Pencavel J., "The Productivity of Working Hours." Discussion Paper No. 8129, April 2014, http://ftp.iza.org/dp8129.pdf.

[xlix] Baumeister R. F., Finkenauer C., Vohs K. D. "Bad is stronger than good." *Review of General Psychology* 2001; 5 (4): 323–370.

[l] Ray R., McRae K., Ochsner K., Gross J. "Cognitive Reappraisal of Negative Affect: Converging Evidence From EMG and Self-Report." *Emotion* 2010; 10 (4): 587–592.

[li] Cabane O. F., *The Charisma Myth: How Anyone Can Master the Art and Science of Personal Magnetism*, 2012.

[lii] Carney D. R., Cuddy A. J., Yap A. J., "Power posing: brief nonverbal displays affect neuroendocrine levels and risk tolerance." *Psychological Science* 2010; 21 (10): 1363–8.

[liii] https://www.vitamindcouncil.org/health-conditions/depression/, Web., October 7th, 2015.